HOW MUCH DO YOU REALLY KNOW ABOUT YOUR CHRISTIAN HERITAGE?

True or false:

—The "Presbyterian Rebellion" was led by the Reverend Dr. John Witherspoon, president of the College of New Jersey (now Princeton) and the only clergyman to sign the Declaration of Independence.

—John Calvin has been called the virtual founder of America.

—The Presbyterians led the American Revolution from the pulpit.

—John Knox almost singlehandedly destroyed the ascendancy of Roman Catholicism in Scotland.

The answers are all "true." And the facts behind them are as compelling as any history ever written.

OUR PRESBYTERIAN HERITAGE is a unique historical and theological survey of Presbyterianism, designed for study, reference, and fascinating reading.

OUR
PRESBYTERIAN
HERITAGE

Paul Carlson

David C. Cook Publishing Co.
850 NORTH GROVE AVENUE • ELGIN, IL 60120
In Canada: David C. Cook Publishing (Canada) Ltd., Weston, Ontario M9L 1T4

OUR PRESBYTERIAN HERITAGE
Copyright © 1973 David C. Cook Publishing Co.

David C. Cook Publishing Co., Elgin, IL 60120

Printed in the United States of America
Library of Congress Catalog Number: 73-86826
ISBN: 0-912692-25-1

To my own sons, Paul and Timothy, elected in the Beloved, and to those other wonderful kids in my confirmation classes at the Glen Morris Presbyterian Church, Ozone Park, New York, this book is affectionately dedicated.

CONTENTS

Foreword

This book is "required" reading for all with whom I am associated in ministry, for every seminarian who interns in our parish, and for the members of the community of faith which I serve as pastor.

It answers a need for a contemporary look at Presbyterian history and theology which I have felt for many years—especially when youth wanted to know the reason for the denomination of which I am a part. I find this book exciting, confirming, informing and deeply satisfying in its relevance to our explosive times and in its healing timeliness for our troubled nation, with its crisis in public affairs, and for a troubled church.

It will not only help Presbyterians to understand their church better, but will give all who read it a more thoughtful understanding of our nation, its genesis, and its profound need now.

For eight years I was a Presbyterian simply because it was in a Presbyterian church where I first found the love of God in Christ and a young pastor, candidating for its pulpit, lovingly and wisely led me to faith in Christ. During subsequent days in college there were great pressures from teachers and peers for me to leave the denomination. Seminary helped to settle me down in the church where I had met the Lord, and though it did not answer all the questions raised by those who had been exerting pressure on me to withdraw, it did much to strengthen me in my persuasion.

But it was four years after ordination and a year after I began to pastor a church that I became a Presbyterian by conviction. As a result of a minor (it seemed major

8

then) crisis in the Presbytery where I was serving, I decided to leave the Presbyterian denomination. Deeply hurt and feeling I had no future in the Presbytery, I began to examine alternatives. The more I examined them, the more convinced I became that there was no system of church government, certainly no theological persuasion to which I would prefer to submit myself. Not that I felt other systems or persuasions were inferior, but simply that I could find none which I preferred to the one in which I had met and been nurtured in Christ.

I wish I had had this book to read in those days. Then it was necessary to search through a number of volumes to find the information and inspiration—and substance—which this one articulate text incorporates.

Once one opens this book and begins to read, he will find it difficult to put it down. It almost reads itself for the reader. From its opening sentences, the argument flows, provokes, virtually seduces the reader to continue. It will inform many Presbyterian readers of many things which they have forgotten. For those for whom the facts are redundant, it will stimulate and excite and awaken to new conviction and commitment. For all it will be confirming and soul satisfying.

It will make Presbyterians proud—not with the pride of the ego—but proud that they stand in the line of such giants of the faith and in a theological persuasion that has had such an incredible impact on history and its empires. It will make Presbyterians grateful that they share such a legacy, and humble as they realize afresh that it is all the work of a sovereign God.

This book speaks to our day, to its disillusionment, as moral crisis faces our nation at its highest levels, to the Church as she struggles with the failure of conventional institutional religion and seeks her way to authentic reformation.

RICHARD C. HALVERSON

For Rebels Only!

THIS BOOK will introduce you to the Presbyterians, as radical and revolutionary a group of men and women who ever lived. In fact, John Calvin was turning the world upside down for Jesus Christ long years before Karl Marx or Che Guevara were ever born.

But what a difference between Calvin's blueprint for revolution and those of later radicals.

The great reformer, like the Master whom he sought to serve, brought the promise of life and freedom. Contemporary revolutionaries have less noble goals. "By their fruits," said Jesus, "you shall know them."

Students today are living in an age when it's fashionable to heap scorn on the so-called "Protestant ethic." They are also bidden to reject the "blind fatalism" of Calvin's theology. Yet the Pied Piper calls them to embrace the historical determinism of Marx, the psychological determinism of Freud, or the "chemical" determinism of the immoral and sadistic de Sade.

Like a foolish Aladdin, they end up trading in the old lamp of the Gospel for the new lamps of unbelief.

It's time to take a look at the Protestant—and Calvinist —heritage of American Christians. For few remember that it was a Presbyterian minister named John Witherspoon who turned the tide in favor of Independence. Or that it was a Presbyterian president who became known as the Great Emancipator, even as he counseled against the harsh judgment of his Southern brethren.

But, more than that, the theology of John Calvin is for Christians who like the "strong meat of the Word." Calvin never ducked the issues. He sought to exhibit the Gospel—and the Christ it presents—in its many facets of beauty.

Some may ask why Calvin is quoted so often. The answer is that most Presbyterians, and even some ministers, betray a shocking ignorance of their faith and the Calvinist tradition.

If you want to know the Bible, read the Bible. If you want to understand Calvinist theology, read the *Institutes* of John Calvin. In neither case be satisfied with secondary sources.

If some words stump you, don't panic. Or get bored. In many cases, a difficult term will be followed by a synonym. For example, the word *labyrinth,* so crucial to an understanding of Calvin's doctrines of God and Scripture, is followed by the word *maze.* Both mean the same thing.

Students may find that the historical section provides some grist for term papers in Reformation and American history. If so, Williston Walker's *A History of the Christian Church* should prove helpful, as well as T. M. Lindsay's two volume *History of the Reformation. The Story of Religion in America* by William Warren Sweet is excellent for studies of the church in the United States.

For those who seek a deeper knowledge of Presbyterian and Reformed theology, the conservative old standbys are works by Charles Hodge, L. Berkhof, and the more recent studies by G. C. Berkouwer.

All of this is to say that, while the most humble and unlettered can know the joy of salvation, a special blessing awaits those who dig into the Bible and theology so that they can give every man a reason for the hope which lies within (I Peter 3: 15). Christianity can still be the religion of an educated mind.

The trouble is that so many want to be spiritual freeloaders. They do so at their own peril. For when the trials strike, they lack those inner resources which prayer and study can alone provide.

It is the author's deepest hope that in these pages you will find the Christ who saves, keeps, and satisfies.

1

The 'Presbyterian Rebellion'

HORACE WALPOLE rose from his seat in the British House of Commons to report on the "extraordinary proceedings" which had lately occurred in the far-off colonies of the New World.

"There is no good crying about the matter," said Walpole sadly. "Cousin America has run off with a Presbyterian parson, and that is the end of it."

That "Presbyterian parson" was none other than the Reverend Dr. John Witherspoon, president of the College of New Jersey (now Princeton University), and the only clergyman to sign the Declaration of Independence.

Walpole had every reason to suspect Witherspoon's personal involvement in this "Presbyterian Rebellion." For none other than George Washington had remarked that, when he took command of the Continental Army in June, 1775, he "abhorred the idea of independence." Thomas Jefferson was similarly inclined as late as August, 1775, when he wrote: "I would rather be in dependence on Great Britain, properly limited, than on any nation on Earth, or than on no nation."

While Jefferson had changed his mind by the time he submitted the Declaration to colonial leaders for approval, the Continental Congress itself hesitated to sign so radical a document.

It was then that Dr. Witherspoon, a lineal descendant of Scotland's fiery preacher-patriot John Knox, rose from his seat to address his wavering comrades.

"There is a tide in the affairs of men," said Witherspoon. "We perceive it now before us. To hesitate is to consent to our own slavery. That noble instrument (The Declaration of Independence) should be subscribed this very morning by every pen in this house."

Witherspoon left no doubt that he himself fully intended to sign that "noble instrument." "For my own part," he declared, "of property I have some, of reputation more. That reputation is staked, that property is pledged on the issue of the contest.

"And although these gray hairs must soon descend into the sepulchre," he added, "I would infinitely rather that they descend thither by the hand of the executioner than desert at this crisis the sacred cause of my country."

Of course, Witherspoon's outright support for the cause of independence was not shared by all clergymen in the colonies. For example, Jonathan Odell, a Tory and an Anglican priest, fled to the British lines in 1777, where he composed snide ditties about the American patriots. Here, in part, is what he wrote about Dr. John Witherspoon:

> To fall by Witherspoon!—O name, the curse
> Of sound religion, and disgrace of verse.
> Member of Congress, we must hail him next:
> "Come out of Babylon," was now his text . . .
> Whilst to myself I've hummed, in dismal tune,
> I'd rather be a dog than Witherspoon.

But the Presbyterian clergy lined up solidly in favor of independence from Great Britain. While a leading Pennsylvania Loyalist informed a British parliamentary committee in 1774 that the Crown's chief opponents were "Congregationalists, Presbyterians and Smugglers," the rector of New York City's famous Trinity Episcopal Church filed this report with the Society for the Propagation of the Gospel in Foreign Parts:

I have it from good authority that the Presbyterian ministers, at a Synod where most of them in the middle colonies were collected, passed a resolve to support the Continental Congress in all their measures. This, and this only, can account for the uniformity of their conduct; for I do not know one of them, nor have I been able, after strict inquiry, to hear of any, who did not, by preaching and every effort in their power, promote all the measures of the Congress, however extravagant.

Some of those early colonial sermons would have shocked those who claim that religion and politics don't mix. For example, when the hated Stamp Act was repealed, a Boston preacher delivered a sermon on the text: "As cold waters to a thirsty soul, so is good news from a far country." Another minister really got in trouble at the outset of the war, when he used for his text: "Better is a poor and wise child, than an old and foolish king, who will no more be admonished." Still later, some thoroughly demoralized Hessian prisoners were treated to a sermon on another text appropos of their situation: "Ye have sold yourselves for naught; and ye shall be redeemed without money."

So great was the power of the Calvinist pulpit during the Revolution that it is said that one fiery New England pastor "preached his whole parish into the army and then to have gone himself."

That this minister was not alone in his strong sentiments toward the war is evident from the distinguished career of George Duffield, pastor of Philadelphia's Third Presbyterian Church, the place where John Adams worshiped during the Continental Congress in 1775. After serving briefly as a chaplain in the disastrous battle of Long Island, Duffield returned home to find his own congregation largely untouched by the war.

"There are too many men in this congregation," he thundered. "There will be one less tomorrow, and no lecture on Wednesday evening."

The hard-nosed George Duffield rejoined Washington's troops once more as a chaplain.

But probably the most engaging story about a patriot-pastor to come out of the Revolutionary War concerns James Caldwell, chaplain to a New Jersey regiment, who was killed by British troops before the war's end. His wife was also slain, and his church burned to the ground.

During a skirmish at Springfield, New Jersey, so the story goes, Caldwell discovered that the Continental forces were running low on wadding for their muskets. So the innovative chaplain ran into a nearby Presbyterian church and picked up an armload of hymnbooks containing the metrical psalms of Isaac Watts. "Now, boys," he cried, "give 'em Watts! Give 'em Watts!"

There were no pacifists—or Tories—in the ranks of the Presbyterians during those decisive years of the nation's history. The gallant "Pennsylvania Line" included six of the early trustees of Pittsburgh's historic First Presbyterian Church, who had become officers in Washington's army. "Similar situations prevailed throughout the colonies," says Gaius Jackson Slosser, "where the patriotic fervor of Presbyterians had become legend."

"When Cornwallis was driven back to ultimate retreat and surrender at Yorktown," writes Thomas Smyth, "all of the colonels of the Colonial Army but one were Presbyterian elders. More than one half of all the soldiers and officers of the American Army during the Revolution were

Presbyterians."

No wonder, then, that a colonist loyal to King George wrote to friends in England: "I fix all the blame of these extraordinary proceedings upon the Presbyterians. They have been the chief and principal instruments in all these flaming measures. They always do and ever will act against government from that restless and turbulent antimonarchial spirit which has always distinguished them everywhere."

However, the Presbyterians paid a heavy price for their involvement in the war. Some of their churches were burned, while others were turned into stables, commissaries, or shelters for the wounded. Pastors were forbidden to preach in areas controlled by the loyalist Anglicans.

At war's end, however, William Warren Sweet records that "no American church was in so deplorable a condition as was the Anglican," which had remained divided over the question of independence throughout the conflict.

Much of the antagonism toward the Anglicans revolved around the fact that they sought to establish an American episcopate in the colonies. So real did this danger seem to both the Congregationalists and the Presbyterians that bishops were viewed as "holy monarchs," who, once established in America, would introduce "canon law—a poison, a pollution." This was the very thing from which the Dissenters had fled in England and on the Continent.

Moreover, the belief was widespread that the Church of England had brought representatives of the Society for the Propagation of the Gospel to America for the sole purpose of "rooting out Presbyterianism." And it did not help the situation when the rector of New York City's Trinity Church wrote to the society's headquarters in England that all of its missionaries remained "opposed (to) the spirit of disaffection and rebellion which has involved this continent in the greatest calamities."

But a new problem arose for the churches immediately following the successful climax of the War of Independence. So great was the respect held for the Presbyterians that members of other denominations feared that the Presbyterian Church would become the Established Church in America.

However, there was no need for alarm. The Presbyterians had suffered for their own faith in Europe, and now they were united in their stand in guaranteeing freedom of conscience for all men. Accordingly, to its everlasting credit, the Presbyterian General Synod in 1783 issued a pronouncement setting forth with clarity its firm view on religious freedom. In part, the General Synod declared:

> It having been represented to Synod, that the Presbyterian Church suffers greatly in the opinion of other denominations, from an apprehension that they hold intolerant principles, the Synod do solemnly and publickly declare, that they ever have, and still do renounce and abhor the principles of intolerance; and we do believe that every member of civil society ought to be protected in the full and free exercise of their religion.

This sense of commitment to human freedom has led many able historians to lavish praise upon our Presbyterian forebears. George Bancroft, for example, declared: "He who will not respect the memory of John Calvin knows nothing of American liberty . . . Calvinism was revolutionary; it taught as a divine revelation the natural equality of man."

Even more pointed is the assessment of an Anglican historian, John Richard Green, author of one of the best histories of the English people. "It is in Calvinism," he says, "that the modern world strikes its roots; for it was Calvinism that first revealed the worth and dignity of man. Called of God, and heir of Heaven, the trader at his counter and the digger in his field suddenly rose in equality with the noble and the king."

Alexis de Tocqueville compared the blatantly antireligious French Revolution to America's War of Independence. "In France I had almost always seen the spirit of religion and the spirit of freedom marching in opposite directions," he wrote. "But in America I found they were intimately united and that they reigned in common over the same country."

A German historian gave the reason for this happy marriage between religion and human freedom. "John Calvin," declared Leopold von Ranke, "was the virtual founder of America."

Those who would question so sweeping a claim must remember that an estimated three million people lived in the colonies at the time of the Revolutionary War. "Of this number," says Egbert Watson Smith, "900,000 were of Scotch or Scotch-Irish origin, 600,000 were Puritan English, while over 400,000 were of Dutch, German Reformed, and Huguenot descent.

"That is to say," explains Dr. Smith, "two thirds of our Revolutionary forefathers were trained in the school of Calvin."

D'Aubigne makes the same claim in his classic *History of the Reformation.* "Calvin was the founder of the greatest of republics," he declared. "The Pilgrims who left their country in the reign of James I, and, landing on the barren soil of New England, founded populous and mighty colonies, were his sons, his direct and legitimate sons; and that American nation which we have seen growing so rapidly boasts as its father the humble Reformer on the shores of Lake Leman (a famous lake in Geneva, Switzerland)."

This thundering theologian of Geneva taught these sons of his that they were subjects of God's electing grace, in all things more than conquerors through the confidence that nothing shall be able to separate them from the love of God in Christ Jesus.

"No doctrine of the dignity of human nature, of the rights of man, of national liberty, of social equality, can create such a resolve for the freedom of the soul as this personal conviction of God's favoring and protecting sovereignty," wrote N. S. McFetridge. "He who has this faith feels he is compassed about with everlasting love, guided by everlasting strength; his will is the tempered steel that no fire can melt, no force can break."

So it is that Presbyterians have clung tenaciously to three fundamental principles of life:

. . . The absolute sovereignty of God.

. . . The absolute equality of clergy and laity.

. . . The absolute solidarity of mankind.

"All of these tenets," says Dr. Slosser, "combine to a concept of life which may be called the divine right of man set over against the obnoxious and iniquitous idea of the divine right of kings." Or as Rudyard Kipling expressed it:

> The people, Lord, the people,
> Not thrones, not crowns, but men.

Presbyterians believe that God alone is the Lord of the conscience, and God alone is the "author of liberty." That is why the "Presbyterian Rebellion" succeeded in America, when the French Revolution degenerated into a tyranny in some ways worse than the one it sought to crush.

Not that those early colonists were any more spiritual or pious than Americans today. Theirs was a cynical and skeptical age not unlike our own. In fact, Increase Mather lamented: "O degenerate New England, what art thou come to this day."

"On the frontier," says Dr. Slosser, "life was crude and callous, a succession of hardships, Indian wars, bereavements, and a monotonous struggle against nature which sought entertaining release in excessive use of liquor and lewd indulgences.

"Educational and religious activities were all too infrequent among the scattered settlers . . ." he records. "Most of them . . . had little more than a nominal contact with the church."

But then something happened in America which shook the very foundations of the soon-to-emerge Republic. It was called "The Great Awakening," which has been described as "the divine answer to the needs of a careless and indifferent age."

Two of the spiritual giants used by God to awaken America out of slumber were Gilbert Tennent, a Presbyterian minister, and George Whitefield, an Anglican by ordination and a close associate of John Wesley in England, who found himself most at home among his Calvinist co-workers in the colonies.

Both of these men were convinced that a *change of heart* preceded a *change in society*. "No one ever became a Christian," Tennent declared, "without first passing through the terror of realizing that he was not a Christian."

In similar fashion, George Whitefield emphasized the need for the New Birth in his preaching tours in New York, Philadelphia, and Boston.

"Why, Mr. Whitefield," inquired a friend one day, "do you so often preach on 'Ye must be born again'?"

"Because," Whitefield replied solemnly, "you must be born again."

The colonists responded to the call of "The Great Awakening" in droves. The fabric of "a carnal society" was reshaped by its force a full generation before the "Presbyterian Rebellion."

And that awakening, tied as it was to a sturdy diet of Calvinist theology, brought about the birth of our nation.

2

Power to the People!

SOME MEN just want to be left alone.

John Calvin, *the* theologian of the Reformation, was one of them.

A shy and stern scholar, Calvin felt much more at home among his beloved books than in the midst of the political and religious upheavals of his own turbulent age.

This unwilling prophet was born of Roman Catholic parents on July 10, 1509, at Noyon, a cathedral town of France, fifty miles northeast of Paris. Since his father hoped that he would one day become a priest, young Calvin was given an "Ivy League" education at the University of Paris and at the famous law school at Orleans.

Already proficient in Latin, philosophy and logic by the time he was fourteen years old, Calvin later studied Greek and Hebrew, eventually writing a commentary on Seneca's Treatise on Clemency. In this book, Calvin quoted from 56 Latin and 22 Greek authors. And he did it without buying the services of Termpapers Unlimited!

Unfortunately, some people who read the commentary on Seneca suspected Calvin of sympathy with the Protestants. Their suspicions turned out to be fully justified when, sometime later, he dropped a theological bombshell upon an already-divided church.

John Calvin's "bomb" came in the form of a little book published initially in 1536, and known to this day as *The Institutes of the Christian Religion*. Although Calvin was only twenty-seven years old when *The Institutes* were first published, the book caused an immediate sensation, and from that moment onward, young Calvin was a marked man.

As the persecutions against the Protestants mounted in France, Calvin decided to leave his homeland and head for that area of Germany where the Reformation had taken root under Martin Luther. In making his travel plans, he concluded that the safest route would be through Switzerland.

God already had "elected" young Calvin for a distinguished—but stormy—career. So when he pulled up to an inn in Geneva in August, 1536, a fiery Protestant by the name of William Farel was on hand to make certain that Calvin canceled his plan to continue his journey the next day.

William Farel had red hair, glittering eyes, and a thunderous voice. And, what's more, he insisted that God had brought John Calvin to Geneva at that providential moment to continue the reformation he had already begun there.

At first, Farel invited Calvin to stay in Geneva. Then he implored. Finally, he called down the wrath of Heaven against this shy young man who begged to be permitted to continue his studies. But let Calvin tell his own story:

Then Farel, finding he gained nothing by entreaties, besought God to curse my retirement and the tranquility of my studies if I should withdraw and refuse to give assistance when the necessity was so urgent. By this imprecation I was so struck with terror that I desisted from the journey I had undertaken; but being sensible of my natural timidity, I would not bring myself under obligations to discharge any particular office.

Young Calvin accepted Farel's impassioned plea, much against his own will, as a divine command to remain in Geneva. "I felt," says Calvin, "as if God from Heaven had laid His mighty hand upon me to stop me in my course."

But the road ahead was not to be easy for the frail and sickly young theologian, who suffered from excruciating headaches. Across the border in France, the Huguenots already were being burned at the stake for their Reformed faith. And, in Geneva itself, there was the constant fear that Catholic forces would, at any moment, march across that border in an attempt to snuff out Protestantism on the shores of Lake Leman.

Moreover, there were enough internal problems in Geneva to try the souls of the best of men. "Sixteenth century manners were generally rough and sixteenth century morals loose," observes T. H. L. Parker. "But Geneva seems to have been rather worse than most towns."

It is not difficult to imagine just how John Calvin reacted to the X-rated abandonment of so many of Geneva's worldly citizens. Nor is it hard to understand just how the city's old and established families felt about the heavy influx of immigrants from other countries who fled to Geneva to escape Catholic persecution in their homelands.

While Calvin quickly addressed himself to the pressing social ills of his adopted city, he often faced some ugly situations because of his desire to turn Geneva into a model City of God on Earth. On more than one occasion, "the only gentleman among the Reformers" heard the unruly mobs outside his window threatening to throw him into the river. No wonder, then, that he later wrote to his fellow pastors in Zurich:

> Although it was a very troublesome province to me, the thought of deserting it never entered my mind. For I considered myself placed in that position by God, like a sentry at his post, from which it would be impiety on my part were I to move a single step. Yet I think you would hardly believe me were I to relate to you even a very small part of those annoyances, nay miseries, which we had to endure for a whole year. This I can truly testify, that not a day passed in which I did not long for death ten times over. But as for leaving that church to remove elsewhere, such a thought never came into my mind.

However, such a thought did come into the minds of Calvin's mounting opposition in the city council and among the rough and rowdy citizens of Geneva who resisted Calvin's heavy-handed law-and-order administration. Finally, he and Farel were forced to flee from the city, Farel never to return again.

Few people today would have liked to live under the oppressive atmosphere of Calvin's Geneva. For prison awaited those who slept in church, gambled for a bottle of wine, criticized a sermon, sang worldly songs, or selected other than Biblical names for their children. People suspected of heresy were either banished or burned.

However, it must be remembered that such coercive uses of government did not originate with John Calvin. They were rather common practice in medieval towns throughout Europe in his day. What he did—erroneously so, from our modern viewpoint—was to baptize such practices with divine blessing.

But the interesting thing is, Calvin was temporarily banished from Geneva not for ruthless government but for attempting to strike a blow for religious freedom! It came about in this way:

In January, 1537, Calvin and Farel appeared before

the city council with a series of recommendations from Calvin's pen. They first suggested that the Lord's Supper be administered monthly in the churches of Geneva. However, they further recommended that the city fathers appoint "certain persons" who, together with the ministers, might report those worthy of church censure, or even excommunication. They also called upon the lawmakers to approve a catechism drafted by Calvin and to impose upon the residents of Geneva a binding creed.

While the city council adopted these measures after considerable modification, trouble had just begun for the two reformers. Individual assent to the new creed aroused bitter opposition in some quarters; and, a year later, the lawmakers bowed to pressure not to deny the Lord's Supper to anyone. What's more, when Calvin's opposition won the next municipal election, it rejected the liturgy used in Geneva for that used in the nearby canton of Bern.

Calvin quickly recognized that a crucial issue was at stake. On the one hand, the decision by the city council to admit all citizens to the sacrament represented a breakdown in church discipline. On the other, the decision of civil authorities to impose a specific liturgy upon Geneva without even consulting the ministers, represented a crushing blow to the freedom of the church.

Therefore, when Calvin and Farel refused to submit to civil authority, they were banished from the city. But already these two men had accomplished more than either of them probably realized. For they had pointed up the absolute necessity of the separation of church and state.

William Farel settled in Neuchatel and never returned to Geneva, while John Calvin went on to Strassburg, a Protestant city of Germany, where he was promptly appointed an assistant professsor of theology. It was also there that he organized a church for French-speaking Protestant refugees. And it was also there that he met and

26

married Idelette de Bure, who has been described as "not only good and honorable but also handsome." So it was that the sovereign God of John Calvin was protecting His servant by a gracious providence even in "the far country."

But things continued to go from bad to worse in Geneva during Calvin's absence. "The immoral element got control, and the moral life of the city became unspeakable," says Walter L. Lingle. "The Roman Catholic Church made a determined effort to overthrow Protestantism. Visitors, strangers, and refugees who had come to Geneva because John Calvin was there ceased to come.

"The people of Geneva began to realize that John Calvin was a great spiritual, moral and financial asset," says Lingle. "There was a growing sentiment for his return."

Finally, in the autumn of 1540, the city council sent an invitation to Calvin by special messenger, urging him to return to Geneva. Thanks, but no thanks, replied Calvin, in a cordial and courteous note.

But the people of Geneva were not satisfied with Calvin's response. "They sent him one invitation after another, and brought great pressure to bear upon him," says Lingle. "They even had William Farel write one of his characteristic letters pronouncing a curse upon him if he did not return."

That was too much for John Calvin. Again, he accepted Farel's thunder as the call of God, and so, on September 13, 1541, returned to Geneva, amid the joyous welcome of a somewhat chastened city.

One of the first things that Calvin did upon his return to Geneva was to secure the adoption of his new *Ordonnances Ecclesiastiques,* which, among other things, sought to widen the breach between church and state. Says Lingle:

Calvin went back to the Bible for everything pertaining to the church—for government, doctrine, worship, discipline and life. When he studied church government in the Bible, he did not find any popes, cardinals, archbishops, and bishops, such as he had known in the Roman Catholic Church from his youth up. Instead he found a church with a very simple form of representative government by elders. He also found in the Bible other church officials called pastors, teachers and deacons. So in the Form of Government drawn up by Calvin there were pastors, elders, deacons, and teachers. When the City Council approved of this Form of Government, the church in Geneva became a Presbyterian church in fact, if not in name. It was called the Reformed Church.

Calvin visualized the roles of these four offices in the following manner: Pastors were to preach, examine candidates for the ministry, and agree on critical matters of Biblical interpretation. Teachers guided the Geneva school system, which Calvin regarded as crucial to the spiritual growth of the city. To the deacons were assigned the care of the poor and the supervision of the hospital. But it was the elders who formed the very heart of Calvin's form of government. They, together with the ministers, made up the *Consistoire,* meeting every Thursday, and charged with ecclesiastical discipline.

This consistory was permitted by law to act in disciplinary matters involving censure and excommunication. However, it was required to refer cases demanding more severe punishment to the civil authorities.

"No right seemed to Calvin so vital to the independence of the church as (that) of excommunication," writes Williston Walker. "And for none was he compelled so to struggle till its final establishment in 1555."

While this consistory embodies some of the rights of a modern Presbyterian session, it was limited in its powers by regulations imposed upon it by civil authorities. For example, the city council remained adamant in its demand that it retain some control over the selection of elders.

The complete separation of church and state still had a long way to go even in the Geneva of John Calvin.

Yet the powers entrusted to the consistory were far-reaching in the area of church discipline. Its members often saw fit to punish those who played cards on Sunday, sang ribald songs, and wasted their time in taverns. They also turned a deaf ear to those who missed compulsory worship services because they had to stay home with children, take care of the cows, or work overtime on the Lord's Day. Such excuses may be accepted today; but in Calvin's Geneva they merited stiff punishment.

Such a stern environment was sure to breed opposition, even though Geneva continued to be flooded by refugees who sought a haven from Roman Catholic persecution. Finally, Calvin faced two crises, between 1548 and 1555, which again threatened his role as the leader of this model community.

The first challenge occurred when a former Parisian monk, Jerome Hermes Bolsec, charged Calvin with doctrinal error because of his teaching on predestination. In the bitter struggle which ensued, Calvin became even more rigid on the matter, and Bolsec himself returned to the Roman Catholic fold, after being banished from Geneva. The final word in the contest came from Bolsec, who wrote a grossly slanderous biography of John Calvin.

Even more unfortunate was Calvin's involvement in the notorious case of Miguel Servetus, a Spaniard of great, though erratic, genius. It is said that Servetus was actually the first to discover the pulmonary circulation of the blood; but he will probably always be remembered as the man who was burned at the stake for heresy while Calvin ruled as the Master of Geneva.

What are the facts?

Servetus, a brilliant lawyer and physician, decided to embark upon the career of a theologian after renouncing the Roman Catholic faith. But rather than casting his lot with the Protestants, he scandalized all Christians by viciously attacking such cardinal doctrines as the deity of Christ, the triune nature of God and the significance of infant baptism. He had also entered into a long and exasperating correspondence with Calvin, whose *Institutes* he had contemptuously criticized.

Acting on evidence supplied by a friend of Calvin, Servetus was arrested by Roman Catholic authorities and condemned by them to the stake. However, he escaped from prison in France, and, for reasons known only to God, made his way to Geneva, even though he had been warned to stay away. To add insult to injury, Servetus demanded that Calvin himself be banished and his worldly goods turned over to him.

What must be remembered is the fact that Calvin's only part in the ultimate condemnation of Servetus came when he appeared as a witness against him. The decision that he be burned at the stake rested upon the city council, of which Calvin was not a member, and which, at that time, was generally hostile to him.

"It is to Calvin's credit that he protested against the burning of Servetus and wanted him decapitated instead," one author observes. "But there is no doubt that he worked for the man's execution and hotly defended it afterward."

While a few voices were raised in protest against the condemnation of Servetus, most men of that turbulent age agreed with the gentle Philip Melanchthon that it was "justly done."

Like all controversial events, the execution of Servetus must be seen against the background of the age in which it occurred. It must be remembered, for example, that, while 58 people were executed and 76 banished during Calvin's tenure in Geneva, 10,220 were burned during that eighteen-year period in which Torquemada headed the Roman Catholic Inquisition.

John Calvin was a man of his own age. And, in that age, he towered above his contemporaries as a statesman, educator, theologian, and, most of all, a minister of the Word of God.

As a statesman, Calvin planted the seeds for freedoms to be enjoyed by later generations. He worked strenuously in Geneva for reforms which still occupy the attention of twentieth-century politicians—full employment, adequate medical and social service benefits, regular garbage collection, urban renewal, and severe penalties for the sale of unhealthy foodstuffs.

As an educator, Calvin organized the Geneva school system, beginning with the primary grades and ending with the Academy, or what is now the prestigious University of Geneva. "We boast of our common schools," says Bancroft of our American public school system. "Calvin was the father of popular education, the inventor of the system of free schools."

As a theologian, Calvin has exercised an influence over the making of the modern mind which few other men have equalled. His theological writings, Bible commentaries, and written sermons fill 48 volumes printed in double column. Duns Scotus may have been called the subtle doctor; Bonaventura, the seraphic doctor; Thomas Aquinas, the angel doctor. But it was John Calvin who was known to the men of his own age as simply *the* theologian.

However, it was as a minister of the Word of God that Calvin sought to be known and remembered. His very first sermon in the Cathedral of St. Pierre created an immediate sensation—because he preached from the Bible. He disliked topical sermons and insisted that Christ's people needed to be exposed to a systematic presentation of the Word. He also abhorred human speculation in either theology or from the pulpit. "When we enter the pulpit," he often declared, "it is not so that we may bring our own

31

dreams and fancies with us." The Bible alone was, for Calvin, the all-sufficient rule for faith and conduct.

For all of his failings, the moral and spiritual magnetism of John Calvin has been recognized by historians and other scholars for 400 years. In fact, the French skeptic and critic, Ernest Renan, willingly testified of this towering theologian: "He succeeded more than all, in an age and in a country which called for reaction towards Christianity, simply because he was the most Christian man of his century."

3

Thunder in the Highlands

THE DIABOLICAL Black Death, which years earlier had swept across Europe like an avenger, was now making another visitation in Montrose and Dundee as George Wishart sought to win a crude and barbarous Scotland for Jesus Christ.

It was a risky business for Wishart to proclaim the Reformed faith in a land which, a few years earlier, had witnessed the death of Patrick Hamilton for engaging in a similar venture.

Wishart himself had earlier been suspected of heresy because he read the Greek New Testament with his students. But now he was leaving no doubt as to where his sympathies rested, as he boldly proclaimed the Gospel of sovereign grace among the rough-hewn Lothians.

So great was the danger for this onetime Cambridge scholar that a young friend stood at his side with a "two-handed sword" as Wishart continued his preaching tour through Montrose, Dundee and Ayrshire.

The name of that young man was John Knox, born near Haddington about 1515, and ordained to the priesthood about twenty-five years later. He became attracted to Wishart because, as Knox was to later write, he was "a man of such graces as before were never heard within this realm, yea, and are rare to be found yet in any man."

But another man had also been attracted by the courageous preaching of George Wishart. His name was Cardinal David Beaton, the thoroughly unscrupulous leader of the Catholic party in Scotland. He immediately conspired for the arrest of this champion of "the new religion," who already was making his impact among the backward Scots.

John Knox remained at the side of his spiritual mentor almost to the bitter end. However, Wishart had a premonition that the end was near; so the night before his arrest, he dismissed the man who would one day carry on his fight for freedom. John Knox did not want to leave. But, said Wishart, "one is sufficient for one sacrifice." Sadly, Knox put away his sword and retreated momentarily into the background.

When Beaton's forces arrived the next day, Wishart was promptly arrested and lodged in the dungeon at St. Andrews. At his later trial, the unsung reformer left no doubt as to what he believed and proclaimed:

... The Holy Scriptures—not fallible councils nor popes—are the test of truth.

... Salvation comes through personal faith in Jesus Christ, not through any sacramental system.

... All men in Christ are priests, not just an exclusive minority ordained by a corrupt church.

Wishart further condemned the Roman Catholic mass as a form of idolatry, and rejected the doctrines concerning priestly celibacy, compulsory confession, the power of exorcism and holy water, and the worship of saints.

With that, his doom was sure. George Wishart was condemned to the stake on March 1, 1546. But, says Harry Emerson Fosdick, "the fire that burned Wishart . . . lit a blaze in Knox which, in the end, destroyed the ascendancy of Roman Catholicism in Scotland."

The rise of papal power, mixed as it was with the political intrigues of the times, came rather late to the shores of Caledonia, as Scotland was originally known among its more civilized neighbors.

While the origins of Celtic Christianity are not entirely known, its relationship to the See of Rome is at best conjectural. It is known, for example, that Columba came from Ireland about 563 A.D. to establish Christian communities, first on the island of Iona, and later on the Scottish mainland. About two centuries after Columba, another Christian movement was established along the eastern coast of Scotland by a group known as the Culdees. But, again, neither Columba nor the Culdees appear to have been in fellowship with the Bishop of Rome.

Roman Catholicism gained a foothold on Scottish soil when Malcolm, a Scottish king, married a beautiful Saxon princess by the name of Margaret, who also happened to be an ardent Catholic. She and her three sons were responsible for leading the Scots away from the ancient faith of Columba and the Culdees and to the binding jurisdiction of the See of Rome. By 1150 A.D. Scotland was completely under the control of papal power.

When the first rays of the Reformation finally dawned on Caledonia, says Thomas McCrie, "the corruptions by which the Christian religion was universally disfigured . . . had grown to a greater height in Scotland than in any other nation within the pale of the Western church."

The grossest forms of superstition were rampant among this rude and ignorant people by the age of Hamilton, Wishart and Knox. Moreover, the Roman Catholic hierarchy itself had degenerated into both moral and spiritual darkness by the time of the Reformation. Such charges are substantiated by the fact that Cardinal Beaton—the man who ordered Wishart's execution—was the father of at least eight illegitimate children.

But apart from Scotland's spiritual darkness there were political considerations which dominated Scottish thinking during the age of John Knox. On the one hand, the Scots had established a strong bond with France, fearing domination or annexation by Great Britain. On the other hand, the British themselves feared such a Scottish-French alliance at the very time they were attempting to make a break with the papacy. "Therefore," says Williston Walker, "England and France both sought to build up parties and strengthen factions favorable to themselves in Scotland."

These facts gain a sense of importance in light of events which occurred shortly after the execution of George Wishart.

For within three months of Wishart's death, Cardinal Beaton himself became the victim of a well-planned assassination. The principal reason behind his murder appears to have been political rather than religious, since Beaton's loyalties were reserved for Catholic France.

Aided by the secret promptings of England, a small band of men broke into the Castle of St. Andrews and slew the cardinal, after which they secured the fortress as a haven for those who sympathized with the English alliance and whose own lives were therefore threatened by supporters of French interests in Scotland.

While John Knox had nothing to do with Beaton's death, he condoned the assassination as a "Godly fact," no doubt mindful of the cardinal's own crimes against Wishart and other Protestants.

Moreover, Knox saw the handwriting on the wall. He knew that he and other Protestants were marked men, that they themselves would be blamed and punished for Beaton's execution unless they escaped from Catholic forces in Scotland.

Knox had thought of taking refuge in Germany. However, he was finally persuaded to join those who had taken over Beaton's own castle at St. Andrews. It was there that Knox, much against his own will, was forced into the role of preacher of the Word of God.

So powerful was the pulpit presence of this sturdy Scotsman that his very first sermon placed him in the ranks of Scotland's foremost reformers. "Others snipped the branches of the papistry," said an early listener. "But he strikes at the root, to destroy the whole."

That such outspoken criticism of Rome would not long be tolerated was indicated by followers of Knox who predicted he would share a fate similar to that of his spiritual mentor. "Master George Wishart spake never so plainly," observed another listener. "And yet he was burnt. Even so will he be."

While John Knox managed to escape execution, he was forced to suffer a living death aboard a French ship after French forces succeeded in battering down the walls of Beaton's castle and compelling the intruders to surrender.

For almost two years, Knox endured the tortures of a galley slave aboard a vessel which once took him past the shoreline of his beloved Scotland. In the distance, he could see the spire of the church in which he once preached. But the sight only deepened his torture, as he realized that he might never stand as a free man on Scotia's shores again.

But a gracious providence was guiding the career of John Knox even as he bent the back to the slavemaster's lash and felt the cast-iron chains dig deeper into his flesh. For it was there in the galley of that enemy ship that this son of Scotland was compelled to learn French—a feat which was to serve him well in God's good season.

At length, an exchange of prisoners brought the release of John Knox. But the still unstable political situation made it impossible for him to return immediately to his own native land.

Therefore, Knox found a haven in England for the next five years. It was there that he served as a minister in Berwick, Newcastle, and London under the protection of the precocious young Protestant king, Edward VI. It was also in England that Knox really began his work as a towering leader of the Reformation.

Edward's death brought to the British throne Mary Tudor, the infamous Bloody Mary, who was soon burning Protestants by the score. Her accession to the throne closed the career of Knox in England, although he continued his ministry there long after his companions had fled to safer quarters. One of his last acts in Britain was to rebuke a crowd for celebrating Mary's entrance into London.

Making his way across the English Channel, John Knox first joined a group of British refugees in Frankfurt. But internal squabbles among them over the Edwardean Prayer Book led Knox to Geneva, where he became an ardent disciple of John Calvin.

It was there by the shores of Lake Leman that Knox learned once more that *all things*—even those torturous months as a galley slave—can "work together for good to them that love God, to them who are the called according to his purpose" (Romans 8: 28).

Had it not been for that crash course in French aboard that slave ship, John Knox would have hardly been able to translate the Reformed theology of John Calvin into the rugged language of the Scottish Highlands.

Calvin, then at the height of his influence in Geneva, had drawn as many as 10,000 Bible students from all over Europe to what has been described as "the most perfect school of Christ that ever was since the days of the apostles." John Knox was just one of those who studied at the feet of this towering French-born and French-speaking theologian.

But John Knox was not content to remain in the largely passive role of a student. He was by nature a man of action. Therefore, he used that time in Switzerland to organize a church for the English-speaking refugees in Geneva. He also sought out other great figures of the Reformation, such as the able and conciliatory Heinrich Bullinger of Zurich, so that he could lay the groundwork for his future campaign against tyranny in Scotland.

Except for a brief visit to his homeland in 1555, John Knox had been in exile for about twelve years when he was summarily called back to Scotland to head up the Reformation there.

"O God," the exile had repeatedly prayed, "Give me Scotland or I die!" That prayer was about to be answered.

In his absence, a number of Protestant and anti-French nobles in Scotland had entered into a covenant to "establish the most blessed Word of God and His congregation." These "Lords of the Congregation," as they came to be known, promised to elect pastors who would "purely and trewlie . . . minister Christis Evangell and Sacramentes to His people."

This act led the Scottish lords to write to Knox, then at Geneva, urging him to return home immediately. Responding to their urgent invitation, Knox arrived in Scotland on May 2, 1559, and immediately set about establishing a church based upon a Presbyterian form of government, such as that found in Calvin's Geneva.

When the first General Assembly of Scotland was convened the following year, Knox submitted a Confession of Faith which was adopted by the Scottish parliament. However, a concession was made to a law which required that only "bishops" could receive certain tax monies.

But the Scots left no doubt that these so-called "bishops" held absolutely no power over the spiritual lives of their people. They called these largely fictional prelates "Tulchan" bishops, a term derived from the effigy of a calf used to lead cows to the milking shed.

John Knox himself was not particularly impressed by this pious and legal fiction. But he went along with the myth of these barnyard bishops so that tax revenues could be diverted to give Scottish youngsters a good Presbyterian education.

Who says the so-called dour Scots don't have a sense of humor? If it was bishops they wanted, bishops they would have!

In actuality, however, the Scottish Reformation recognized that Protestantism and national independence were bound together. On the one hand, the despotic James VI of Scotland was forced to concede: "Presbytery agreeth as well with monarchy as God and the devil." On the other hand, the egalitarian Scots themselves were willing to give the devil his due. "There may be a place for bishops," they magnanimously agreed, "but *not* in the Church of Scotland!"

The Book of Discipline compiled under the leadership of John Knox was one of the most remarkable documents of that age. It provided for the government of the church by sessions, synods, and the General Assembly. "The individual church was to have a pastor, elders and deacons," Walter Lingle notes. "The elders and deacons were to be elected for only one year at a time, 'lest that by long continuance of such officers men presume upon the liberty of the church.' "

But the Book of Discipline did not confine its attention to the matter of church government. It also decreed that every congregation was to establish a school for the teaching of Latin, grammar and the catechism. Provision was further made for high school and college training for every lad capable of such study. Thus the groundwork had been laid in both Geneva and Edinburgh for what was to become a hallmark of Presbyterian faith and life—an educated ministry and an equally educated laity.

These early Presbyterians had immersed themselves in Scripture, if not in water! They passionately believed that "the entrance of thy words giveth light; it giveth understanding unto the simple" (Psalm 119: 130). They further resisted both prelate and crown in the firm belief that "ye shall know the truth, and the truth shall make you free" (John 8: 32).

Yet it was a Calvinist scholar of a much later generation who once remarked that he was first attracted to the Gospel because, he said, "Christianity is the religion of an educated mind."

Moreover, those early Presbyterians insisted that Christian faith and Christian action go hand-in-hand. Therefore, the Book of Discipline also established a code of conduct for a people that were once known to be about as unruly as any in Europe.

The Scottish Confession of Faith, for example, left no doubt as to how Christianity should express itself in everyday life: "To save the lives of innocents, to repress tyrannies, to defend the oppressed, to keep our bodies clean and holy, to live in soberness and temperance, to deal justly with all men both in word and deed, and to repress all appetite of our neighbor's hurt, are the good works . . . which are most pleasing and acceptable to God."

"Knox made Calvinism the religion of Scotland, and Calvinism made Scotland the moral standard for the world," says Egbert Watson Smith. "It is certainly a significant fact that in that country where there is the most of Calvinism there should be the least of crime; that of all the peoples of the world today that nation which is confessedly the most moral is also the most thoroughly Calvinistic; that in that land where Calvinism has had supremest sway individual and national morality has reached its loftiest level."

Critics may argue that Calvinism doesn't seem to be doing very well in the personal and public morals arena today. But this is not the fault of Calvinism as much as that of the sons of the Calvinists, who have abandoned "the faith which was once delivered unto the saints" (Jude 3).

Those sturdy Scotsmen of a bygone age believed that the Christian religion should dominate every area of the lives of both men and nations. They would have nothing to do with that heresy that religion and politics don't mix. John Knox himself was plunged, as Dr. Fosdick points out, into "the rough and tumble of politics, so that his major meaning lies in what he did, rather than in what he wrote."

It must be remembered that Scotland had her own king and her own parliament until 1603, when James VI of Scotland became James I of England. It was during the reign of the king's mother, the tragic Mary Queen of Scots, that the career and prestige of John Knox reached its pinnacle of spiritual and political power.

In fact, the young and beautiful Mary had returned to Scotland from France in August, 1561—just one year almost to the day after the Scottish parliament had hearkened to the persuasive voice of John Knox and rejected Roman Catholicism in favor of the Reformed faith as the established religion of the land.

Mary Stuart, an ardent Catholic, had hardly settled in Holyrood Palace in Edinburgh when she celebrated mass, against the new law of the Scottish parliament. When John Knox heard of the incident, he declared from the pulpit that one mass frightened him more than 10,000 enemy soldiers.

Mary, in turn, heard about that famous sermon and summoned the Great Thunderer to the palace to give an account of himself. How dare he transgress God's law, Mary asked, by enjoining her subjects to disobey the commands of their sovereign?

John Knox stood firm against Mary's feminine wiles and Mary's royal threats. Declared the unbending reformer:

> As right religion took neither original strength nor authority from worldly princes, but from the eternal God alone, so are not subjects bound to frame their religion according to the appetites of their princes. For oft it is that princes are the most ignorant of all others in God's true religion . . .

> If all the seed of Abraham had been of the religion of pharaoh, whose subjects they long were, I pray you, madam, what religion would there have been in the world? Or if all men in the days of the apostles had been of the religion of the Roman emperors, what religion would there have been upon the face of the earth?

"And so, madam," declared Knox, "ye may perceive that subjects are not bound to the *religion* of their princes, albeit they are commanded to give them obedience."

But, Mary replied, "ye interpret the Scriptures in one manner, and they (the Roman Catholic teachers) interpret in another. Whom shall I believe, and who shall be judge?"

Retorted the reformer: "Ye shall believe God, that plainly speaketh in His Word, and farther than the Word teaches you, ye shall neither believe the one nor the other.

"The Word of God is plain in itself; and if there appear any obscurity in one place, the Holy Ghost, which is never contrary to Himself, explains the same more clearly in other places, so that there can remain no doubt but unto such as obstinately remain ignorant."

"The Kirk of Rome," declared Mary finally, "is the one I will obey."

The issue which divided these two strong willed personalities is as fresh as tomorrow's newspaper. Does the church have the right, after all, to disobey duly constituted civil authority?

John Calvin had emphasized in theocratic Geneva that "one cannot resist magistrates without resisting God." And, on this point, he could cite no less an authority than St. Paul, who declared: "Let every soul be subject unto the higher powers. For there is no power but of God" (Romans 13: 1ff). In similar fashion, Peter admonished: "Submit yourselves to every ordinance of man for the Lord's sake: whether it be to the king, as supreme; or unto governors, as unto them that are sent by him for the punishment of evildoers, and for the praise of them that do well" (I Peter 2: 13, 14).

John Knox, however, was forced by a despotic monarchy to emphasize an equally valid strand of Biblical truth. There was never a doubt in his mind that, if there was a "divine right of kings," there was also a "divine right of presbyteries." And when these rights came into conflict, the latter determined the course of correct action for the man of God.

"The prophet of God," declared Knox, "sometimes may teach treason against kings, and yet neither he, nor such as obeys the word spoken in the Lord's name by him, offends God."

In the end, Mary's own folly and misdeeds brought about her downfall. She was forced to abdicate her crown and flee the country. Alienated from her onetime supporters, and personally involved in a plot against the life of England's Protestant Queen Elizabeth, Mary was at length jailed and later executed in Lochleven Castle. Her infant son, James VI, succeeded her on the throne.

As for John Knox, his last years were limited by broken health, a testimony to his continuing struggle against those opponents whom he called "the bloody, butcherly brood."

He was a tough man for a tough age; and, when he died in 1572, Regent Morton stood by his open grave, and said simply and finally: "Here lies one who never feared the face of man."

4

They Dared to Be Different

CARACCIOLO, a Neopolitan noble in the service of Emperor Charles V, was a broken man when he was only thirty-five years old.

He had been the happily married father of six children when he embraced the Reformed faith of John Calvin. He had known that such a radical step could result in his losing his position and wealth, if not his life. Yet Caracciolo dared to be different.

However, his wife and children wanted no part in his scheme to flee Naples and resettle in Calvin's Geneva. They were ardent Roman Catholics and were as unwilling to live in a Protestant country as he was to remain in Catholic Italy.

Caracciolo's father, a relative of the pope, had hoped that an arrangement could be worked out so that the family could be reunited in Venice, where each member would be left to practice his own religion.

But the plan was foiled when Caracciolo's wife steadfastly refused to see her husband, much less follow him into a strange and new life. At length, he decided to risk his life by making a secret visit home in a last-ditch effort to preserve his marriage.

It was a happy homecoming because the family thought that Caracciolo had returned to his senses and was home to stay. But when they discovered that he had come home only to win them over to evangelical faith, the father cursed, the wife wept, and the twelve-year-old daughter grabbed both feet in a childlike attempt to keep her daddy home.

Caracciolo was almost reduced to tears himself. But he knew that the price for regaining his home involved the abandonment of his new faith. And this was a price he refused to pay.

Sadly, Caracciolo returned to the boat, torn by the tragic sight of his wife and children standing on the shore and begging him to stay.

Little is known about this family which was broken apart by a set of beliefs for which thousands upon thousands of men and women were willing to die. Caracciolo himself became an elder in the Italian church at Geneva.

So wrecked did Europe become by the series of religious wars which followed in the wake of the Reformation that human sensibilities are still shocked by the excesses on both sides. Protestants destroyed Catholic churches and wore necklaces fashioned out of the severed ears of priests, while a Roman Catholic commander once asked his men: "Why do you crowd the prisons with Protestant captives? Is the river full?"

There are many lessons to be learned by Christians today as they reflect upon the differences between the Reformation Age and our own day when so many believe that it doesn't matter what you believe just as long as you believe something.

The study of the Reformation period is long and tedious. Therefore, only a few vignettes—or snapshots—can be introduced to show that our Protestant forefathers were fighting battles which still have not been fully settled. They knew that faith and freedom go hand-in-hand.

One of the blackest days in church history occurred on August 24, 1572, when thousands of French Calvinists, known as Huguenots, were murdered by Catholic forces in what became known as the Massacre of St. Bartholomew's Day.

The Protestants had been lured to Paris by the thoroughly unscrupulous Catherine de Medici, who had arranged a marriage of political convenience between her daughter Marguerite and a young Protestant leader, King Henry of Navarre. The hope had been that such a marriage would end religious warfare in France.

But that was not to be.

The great bell of the Cathedral of St. Germain began to toll just before dawn on August 24th, signaling the massacre which was to sweep throughout France. One of those killed was Admiral Gaspard de Coligny, the beloved Huguenot leader, who embraced the Reformed faith after studying the Scriptures and receiving the encouragement of none other than Calvin himself.

The assassin first plunged a sword through Coligny's body, which was then thrown out of a window. Finally, to make certain that he had died, the great leader of the Protestant cause was decapitated.

There is little question that politics played as great a role as religion in the St. Bartholomew's Day Massacre. For the Huguenots, not unlike their Scottish co-religionists, favored local autonomy over monarchy. Coligny's popularity among the Protestants made him especially hated by the notorious Catherine.

"When news of the massacre reached Rome," says one historian, "the exultation among the clergy knew no bounds. The cardinal of Lorraine rewarded the messenger with a thousand crowns; the cannon of St. Angelo thundered forth a joyous salute; and bells rang out from every steeple; bonfires turned night into day; and Gregory XIII, attended by the cardinals and other ecclesiastical dignitaries, went in long procession to the church of St. Louis, where the cardinal of Lorraine chanted a Te Deum . . ."

The roots of the Reformation in France were buried in shallow and rocky ground from that day in 1572, when a noted humanist by the name of Jacques Lefevre dared to write: "It is God who gives us, by faith, that righteousness which by grace alone justifies to eternal life."

Lefevre, once a dedicated Romanist, had reached this conclusion before the days of either Luther or Zwingli, as he sought to "preach Christ from the sources," namely, the Bible. In his study, Lefevre anticipated two ideas of the later Reformers: justification by grace apart from good works, and the "real presence" of Christ in the Lord's Supper apart from the Roman dogma of transubstantiation.

Lefevre and other early French evangelicals were men before their times. They earnestly yearned for reform; but they abhorred the very notion of rebellion. Yet a full generation before the first Protestant church was founded in France in 1555, Roman Catholic officials had been quick to recognize the political dangers of the new religious spirit.

"This mania," the pope assured the regent of France, "will not only confound and destroy religion, but all principalities, nobility, laws, orders, and ranks beside."

A few years later, a papal nuncio warned the king: "Sire, be not deceived. The Protestants will upset all civil as well as religious order . . . The throne is in as much danger as the altar . . . The introduction of a new religion must necessarily introduce a new government."

The spirit of liberty, Rome correctly foresaw, went

hand-in-hand with the Bible.

Therefore, the Lefevre translation of the Scriptures was put to the flames. But, in the providence of God, that Word did not return unto Him void. For one of Lefevre's students was none other than William Farel, who was responsible for bringing the Gospel and Calvin to Geneva!

France never fully recovered from the persecutions it visited upon the Protestants. It has been estimated that as many as four million were lost by flight or martyrdom.

Even the rationalist historian William E. H. Lecky saw that the loss of the Huguenots to France was irreparable. "It prepared the way," he says, "for the inevitable degradation of the national character and removed the last serious bulwark that might have broken the force of that torrent of skepticism and vice, which, a century later, laid prostrate in merited ruin, both the altar and the throne."

Lecky was of course referring to the bloody French Revolution, which followed on the heels of the American War of Independence. But unlike that of the colonists, the French Revolution was bathed in a deeply antireligious spirit, a spirit which gave birth to the September massacres and the Reign of Terror. So great were the atrocities committed that H. G. Wells was forced to say of the more radical revolutionists: "There was something inhuman even in their humanitarian zeal."

Meanwhile, the teachings of Martin Luther found their way into Holland and Belgium at an early date. But it was the theology of John Calvin which was to make the deepest and most lasting impression upon the people of the Netherlands.

So quickly did the Reformed faith spread through these two countries that, by 1531, twenty-five translations of the Bible were available in Dutch, Flemish, and French. To own or read one, however, meant certain death. In fact, in July, 1523, Henry Voes and John Esch were burned in Brussels for embracing Protestant beliefs.

These persecutions were most intense just at the time when William the Silent, Prince of Orange, became the military and political leader of the Protestant cause in the Netherlands. Under his leadership, the seven northern provinces were welded into the Dutch Republic in 1579.

That was twenty years after a student of Calvin's arrived from Geneva to organize the first church and draw up what has become known as the Belgic Confession of Faith. Then, in 1569, the Presbyterians of the Netherlands, unable to meet in their own country because of persecution, convened in Emden, Germany, to organize a synod based upon a constitution adopted six years earlier.

Like the Presbyterians of France and Switzerland, those in the Netherlands ultimately adopted the name of the Reformed Church. But that was in name only. They embraced the theology of John Calvin and organized themselves under a Presbyterian form of government.

But there was room for innovation. As the Scottish church decided to elect elders and deacons for only one year, the Dutch introduced the concept of the collegiate church, under which all of the congregations in a given city were governed by one session.

Some of these collegiate churches were established at an early date in the New World, the most famous of which is Marble Collegiate Church in New York City, where the Reverend Dr. Norman Vincent Peale has served as pastor for many years. They are affiliated with the Reformed Church in America, which claims to be the nation's oldest denomination, finding its origin in the establishment of a collegiate church in New Amsterdam under the leadership of Dominie Jonas Michaelius in 1628.

Meanwhile, back in the Netherlands, a feud was boiling which was to reach its climax in the Arminian controversy at the University of Leyden in 1603. The battle continued for years to come.

At the center of the controversy stood a professor

named Jacob Arminius, who protested against the hyper-Calvinism of many of his colleagues. He particularly singled out what unfortunately became known as the Five Points of Calvinism, or the Gospel in a T-U-L-I-P (These are discussed in the chapter entitled "The Gospel in a T-U-L-I-P"):

Total depravity.
Unconditional election.
Limited atonement.
Irresistible grace.
Perseverance of the saints.

So hot did this contest become that the government itself convened the Synod of Dort, named after the town in which it met. The synod, which held sessions between November, 1618, and the following May, ultimately condemned the Arminian preachers and banished them from the country.

The so-called Canons of the Synod of Dort, the Belgic Confession of Faith and the Heidelberg Catechism, remain the doctrinal standards of the Dutch Reformed Church to this day.

While most synod members were Dutch, delegates came from other countries as well. Those who came from the Anglican Church of England were instructed by James I to try to "mitigate the heat on both sides."

The British crown wisely understood that, while scholars might sometimes debate the more obtuse points of theology, the man in the streets just wants to hear the simple message of God's redeeming love in Christ.

Not that James I was any particular friend of the Presbyterians. Quite the reverse is true.

England had broken with Rome during the reign of Henry VIII, when a dispute with the pope over the king's personal life led Henry to proclaim himself head of the Church of England in temporal affairs. Religious matters were left to Thomas Cranmer, the Archbishop of Canterbury, who shared some of the views of the reformers.

However, Henry had earlier been declared a *Fidei Defensor,* a Defender of the Faith, by the pope because of a tract he had written against the teachings of Martin Luther. So it is not surprising that he retained the government and general doctrinal system of the Roman Catholic Church when the break occurred in 1534.

At the same time, some progress was made under the spiritual leadership of Thomas Cranmer. The English Bible was placed in all of the churches, and the Thirty-Nine Articles were introduced as the doctrinal standard of the Anglican Communion. Moreover, the first edition of the beloved Book of Common Prayer made its way into English-speaking hearts during this stormy period.

But the major change was to be found in Henry's Act of Supremacy, which gave legal standing to his break with Rome. While most Britons supported the measure, others did not.

One of Henry's detractors was the distinguished Sir Thomas More, who flatly refused to buy the argument that the king was the head of the church simply because Parliament said so. His wit remained with him right to the scaffold. "See me safe up," he told an officer. "I'll take care of myself coming down!"

When Henry died in 1547, he was succeeded on the throne by his nine-year-old son, Edward VI. But his reign was short lived, and Bloody Mary was crowned as sovereign of England. She promptly proceeded to return Great Britain to the Roman Catholic fold.

Thomas Cranmer and other leading bishops were burned at the stake. Two of them were Hugh Latimer and Nicholas Ridley. As they faced death together in 1555 at Oxford, Latimer turned to Ridley as the flames licked their prey, and said firmly: "Be of good cheer, brother Ridley, and play the man, for we shall this day light such a candle by God's grace in England, as I trust shall never be put out."

Though a bishop himself, Latimer had inflamed many against him with words such as these from his pulpit at Worcester: "Who is the most diligent bishop and prelate in all England? . . . I will tell you: it is the devil . . . He is never out of his diocese . . .

"Where the devil is resident . . . there away with books, and up with candles; away with Bibles, and up with beads; away with the light of the Gospel, and up with the light of candles . . . Down with Christ's Cross, up with purgatory pickpurse . . . Away with clothing the naked, the poor, and impotent, up with decking of images . . . Up with man's traditions and his laws, down with God's traditions and His most Holy Word . . ."

None of these martyrs were Presbyterians. They, rather, belonged to the Church of England. Yet they shared many of the same longings as their Scottish brethren, and suffered with them for the Gospel of Christ.

Some of them who escaped the fate of men such as Latimer and Ridley fled to Geneva during Mary's reign. There they joined the English-speaking congregation of none other than John Knox.

After Mary's death, in 1558, Elizabeth ascended the throne as Queen of England, beginning a reign which was to last until 1603. Three years later, Mary Stuart arrived from France as Queen of Scotland. Mary was the ardent Catholic, while Elizabeth reaffirmed the Act of Supremacy and restored Protestantism in England.

With the return of the Protestant exiles, efforts were made to impose upon the Church of England a more Scriptural form of life and worship. These reformers therefore gained the nickname of Puritans, although they were nothing other than zealous Calvinists.

While Elizabeth sought to make these Puritans conform to the discipline of the English church, the noted historian John Richard Green has observed that they completely altered the moral and spiritual life of the nation. "England became the people of a book," says Green, "and that book was the Bible."

However, new trials faced the Calvinists of England and Scotland when Elizabeth died. Her crown was passed to James VI of Scotland, son of Mary Queen of Scots. He thereby became James I, King of England and Scotland, and the two nations became united under one sovereign.

The Calvinists of both countries held high hopes that the ascension of James would bring an end to religious persecution and warfare in the United Kingdom, since the new king had been educated by the Presbyterians in Scotland. But they were to be sadly disappointed.

"I will make them conform," said James of the English Puritans. "Or I will harry them out of the land or worse!"

"He did harry some of them out of the land," says Walter Lingle. "They came to Plymouth Rock and New England, and thus enriched the spiritual life of America. But James never succeeded in his efforts to make them conform.

"They were stronger at his death," he says, "than they were at the beginning of his reign."

But that does not mean that James did not try to make life unbearable for these Presbyterians and other nonconformists.

In Scotland, for example, the scholarly Andrew Melville, the successor to John Knox, seized the king by the robe on one occasion, and declared: "Sir, as divers times before I have told you, so now again I must tell you, there are two kings and two kingdoms in Scotland: there is King James, the head of the Commonwealth, and there is Christ Jesus, the King of the Church, whose subject James is, and of whose kingdom he is not a king, nor a lord, nor a head, but a member.

"We will yield to you your place, and give you all due obedience," Melville added. "But again I say that you are not the head of the Church!"

It is not surprising that Melville was first imprisoned, then banished from the country for his outspoken candor. Yet it was later said of him: "Scotland never received a greater benefit at the hands of God than this man."

In England, meanwhile, James had published a *Book of Sports* "to encourage recreation and sports on the Lord's Day." Its publication brought an immediate outcry from the Puritans, who opposed the frivolity of the times, and sought to promote a stricter observance of the Christian day of rest.

James reacted to such opposition by attempting to kill two birds with one stone. Ireland had refused to break with Rome at the time of Henry VIII, unleashing a series of religious wars which had practically depopulated Northern Ireland by the end of Elizabeth's reign in 1603.

James attempted to solve this Irish problem, a problem which he inherited, by following the advice of Francis Bacon and establishing "The Ulster Plantation" in that decimated land. It was a decision which was to haunt the British down to the present day.

While the king forcibly deported many of his outspoken critics to Ulster, there was a great migration of Presbyterians from the Scottish lowlands who settled in Northern Ireland. But there were also some among them who were nothing other than profane, rough-hewn adventurers.

However, a great revival soon swept the Ulster Plantation under the powerful preaching of men such as the Reverend James Glendinning, who, as a writer of the time observed, "would never have been chosen by a wise assembly of ministers, nor sent to begin a reformation in this land." He preached nothing but law, wrath, and the terrors of God, until people under conviction swooned away, at last begging to know, "What must we do to be saved?"

Meanwhile, when James died in 1625, he was succeeded by his son, Charles I, who was even more determined than his father to make the Puritans of England and the Presbyterians of Scotland conform to the Anglican form of worship and church government. He found a vigorous ally in this effort in the person of William Laud, the Archbishop of Canterbury.

The day came, July 23, 1637, when the Dean of Edinburgh entered St. Giles Church—the church of John Knox —and attempted to conduct divine worship according to Archbishop Laud's prayer book, decreed by the king as binding upon all Christians in the realm.

The poor dean was met by a flying stool, hurled at him by Jenny Geddes, a Scottish working woman. Pandemonium broke out, and the officiating clergyman was forced to head for the Highlands, ducking other missiles in his hasty retreat.

But the Scottish Presbyterians knew that they would have to pay dearly for failing to follow their own rubric of doing "all things decently and in order." So they bound themselves together by a National Covenant, pledging to stand by one another until death. Many signed the document in their own blood.

In Ireland, meanwhile, the notorious Thomas Wentworth went about the dirty business of forcing Anglican discipline upon both the Roman Catholics and the Presbyterians of that unhappy land. He demanded that the latter swear "upon the Holy Evangelists" to renounce all Scottish covenants and subscribe to what became known as the Black Oath. Many refused and were forced to flee for their lives. Others were imprisoned in dungeons.

Ireland's troubles were only beginning. Wentworth was eventually recalled because of his oppressive rule. But then, after only a few years of relative calm, new atrocities were visited upon the Presbyterians of Ulster. This time the enemy proved to be the native Irish Catholics, who waged a massacre against the Protestants in 1641, which rivaled only the bloodbath of St. Bartholomew's Day in France less than a century earlier.

About this same time, however, Charles' excesses were proving to be his own undoing. His forays against the Scots for rejecting Anglican discipline ended in defeat and an empty treasury.

The king had been ruling for some time without the aid of a parliament. Now he was forced to call for the election of one to vote him men and money. To his horror, two successive parliaments were elected, the second with a larger Puritan majority than the first. In the end, Charles lost his head, and the parliamentary forces established a commonwealth under the leadership of Oliver Cromwell. England and Scotland had no king for the next eleven years.

At last the hour had struck for the Puritans to introduce those reforms of the spirit for which they had worked and waited for seventy-five years. Their opportunity came when the parliament itself convened what has become known in history as the Westminster Assembly of Divines, which held its first session in Westminster Abbey, London, on July 1, 1643. These meetings were to continue for the next five and a half years.

The assembly itself was composed of 121 of England's most able ministers, 20 members of the House of Commons, and 10 members of the House of Lords. Scotland was invited to send six commissioners, who exercised an influence upon the assembly out of all proportion to their numbers.

In the end, participants presented to the world a series of documents which were ultimately rejected by the Church of England, but warmly embraced by the Presbyterians of Scotland and other nations. Among them were the Westminster Confession of Faith and the Larger and Shorter Catechisms.

There was even a period of about twelve years in

which the Presbyterian Church was recognized as the established church of England. But then came the Restoration of the monarchy under Charles II, and "The Great Ejectment" of Calvinism in England.

However, word was being received by the beleaguered Calvinists of Scotland, Ireland, and England of a great Zion in the Wilderness in the New World. The name of this Promised Land was America!

5

Zion in the Wilderness

THE REVEREND FRANCIS MAKEMIE, the acknowledged "Father of American Presbyterianism," would have probably flunked the Dale Carnegie course.

Makemie may not have won many friends. But he sure did influence a lot of very important people, if only negatively.

One man who bitterly resented this young Ulster minister was Lord Cornbury, the corrupt Governor of New York, who dismissed Makemie as "a Jack-of-all-trades, a preacher, a doctor of physic, a merchant, an attorney, a counselor-at-law, and, which is worst of all, a disturber of governments."

There is no doubt that Makemie was a man of many talents. He had a genius for leadership and organization and invested the returns from his business ventures to finance the costs of running a parish that extended all the way from Barbados to New York! "His diverse gifts," says Dr. Slosser, "ideally fitted him for rugged service over a far-flung frontier."

Moreover, Makemie's knowledge of British law was to serve this "Jack-of-all-trades" well when Lord Cornbury had him and a colleague, John Hampton, jailed as "strolling preachers," who had dared to preach without his approval.

It must be remembered that Anglicanism represented the established church in most of the colonies in those days. Religious liberty was still far from a reality in British-dominated America.

Makemie and Hampton were therefore arrested on orders of Cornbury as soon as they set out on what may be called the first "moderatorial tour" by Presbyterian leaders in America. Their journey followed the organization of the Presbytery of Philadelphia in 1706, a meeting attended by ministers from Maryland, Delaware and eastern Pennsylvania.

With characteristic courage, Makemie informed the governor: "If your Lordship requires it, we will give security for our behavior. But to give bond and security to preach no more in your excellency's government, if invited and desired by any people, we neither can nor dare do it."

Cornbury responded to such outspoken talk by allowing Makemie and Hampton to languish in jail without bail for almost two months. When they finally were released on bond, a group of New England Puritans immediately sprang to their defense, writing a strong letter of protest to England and making certain that their brethren were well-prepared for their forthcoming trial.

Testifying in his own defense, Makemie answered Cornbury's charges point by point. "My license which I got in England as a dissenter," argued Makemie, "is good in all Her Majesty's dominions . . . including New York."

A jury ultimately acquitted the two clergymen of all

charges pending against them. However, the spiteful governor compelled Makemie to pay the entire trial costs, not only of his own defense, but of the prosecution as well. "These costs amounted to the large sum of more than 83 pounds," says Dr. Slosser. "It was more than a minister's salary would be for an entire year."

Sadly, the imprisonment and trial had taken a heavy toll on the strength of Francis Makemie. He died the following year at the comparatively young age of fifty. But not before he had struck a resounding victory for freedom of religion and speech throughout the colonies.

The Presbytery of Philadelphia, of which Makemie was the first moderator, celebrated its 200th anniversary in 1906. On that historic occasion, a poetic tribute was paid to the "Father of American Presbyterianism" by Henry van Dyke:

To thee plain hero of a rugged race,
We bring a meed of praise too long delayed.
Oh, who can tell how much we owe to thee
Makemie and to labors such as thine
For all that makes America the shrine
Of faith untrammeled and of conscience free?
Stand here, gray stone, and consecrate the sod
Where sleeps this brave Scotch-Irish man of God.

Actually, Presbyterian faith reportedly was planted in the New World by the Reverend Alexander Whittaker, whom Bancroft calls "the self-denying Apostle of Virginia." He arrived in America in 1611, just four years after the settlement of Jamestown.

Although the Pilgrims and the Puritans were strict Calvinists, most of them favored a congregational form of church government. But there were some Presbyterians among them.

In addition, the fires of persecution in Europe brought waves of Calvinists from other countries to the New World at an early date. Among them were French Huguenots,

Germans, and Dutch. They called themselves Reformed; but that was in name only. For all of them embraced the Presbyterian system of government.

But it was left to the Scotch and the so-called Scotch-Irish to make the most indelible imprint upon the emerging Presbyterian Church in America. It has been conservatively estimated that, between 1705 and 1775, at least 500,000 of these Ulster Irish had settled in the colonies. (The Scotch-Irish didn't have a drop of Irish blood in their veins. They were Scotsmen who lived in North Ireland before immigrating to America.)

"The great tide of Scotch-Irish immigration set in just about the time the first presbytery was organized," says Dr. Lingle. "And the Presbyterian Church began to grow rapidly."

About a decade after Makemic had organized the Presbytery of Philadelphia, seventeen ministers and several ruling elders attended the first meeting of the Philadelphia Synod, which was composed of four presbyteries. Things appeared to be looking up.

But then internal strife hit the Presbyterians with a vengeance.

These early churchmen had weathered the question of whether the Westminster Confession of Faith and Catechisms should be made binding upon all Presbyterian ministers. They did so by reaching a compromise in the Adopting Act of 1729, which demanded unity in essential doctrine, but freedom of conscience in all other matters.

While a minister was expected to withdraw from the Presbyterian Church if the presbytery or synod adjudged his doctrinal position at variance with the denomination, the Adopting Act declared:

The synod do solemnly agree that none of us will traduce or use any opprobrious terms of those who differ from us in these extra-essential and not necessary points of doctrine, but treat them with the same friendship, kindness and brotherly love, as if they had not differed from us in such sentiments.

But trouble still loomed ahead for the infant church. Ironically, the division occurred not because of doctrinal differences but over the questions of evangelism and education. Says Dr. Lingle:

> In 1741, the Synod of Philadelphia split into Old Side and New Side. The New Side withdrew and, in 1745, organized the Synod of New York. So from 1741 to the reunion in 1758, there were two separate and distinct Presbyterian churches in America. One was the Old Side Synod of Philadelphia and the other the New Side Synod of New York.

The Great Awakening was sweeping across the colonies at this time under the leadership of George Whitefield. His evangelistic preaching had won the wholehearted support of a group of younger Presbyterian ministers, led by the Reverend Gilbert Tennent.

However, many of the older Scotch and Scotch-Irish ministers objected to the "new enthusiasm" and Whitefield's aggressive evangelism. Tennent himself only poured salt into the wounds of these men by preaching a sermon entitled "The Unconverted Ministry."

At the same time, the situation was aggravated by differences over the question of the proper education of the ministry. The Old Side believed that pastors should either be trained in England or Scotland or at Harvard or Yale. The New Side insisted that the sharp rise in church membership, brought about in part by the revivals, demanded that some other plan be devised to meet the pressing need for more ministers.

To meet this need, the Reverend William Tennent, father of Gilbert Tennent, began to train many young men for the ministry at his school at Neshaminy, Pennsylvania, near Philadelphia, which his opponents derisively called

"The Log College." Graduates of this school were to make their impact upon the Presbyterian Church for years to come.

The breach between these two "sides" of the church was finally healed in 1758, when the Synod of New York and Philadelphia was established. There followed a great period of missionary expansion, which was in full swing when John Witherspoon arrived from Paisley, Scotland, in 1768, to assume his duties as president of the College of New Jersey.

Even before the end of the Revolutionary War, plans were underway to divide the far-flung synod into more manageable geographical units. Accordingly, the synods of New York and New Jersey, Philadelphia, Virginia and the Carolinas were formed, looking forward to the first meeting of the Presbyterian General Assembly on May 21, 1789 at Philadelphia—just three weeks after George Washington was inaugurated the first President of the United States.

Both the Presbyterians and the Congregationalists enjoyed widespread popular support after Independence because of their wholehearted participation in the war. Therefore, in 1801, these two Calvinistic bodies entered into a cooperative union with mutual exchange of ministers to meet the ever-growing demands of the movement Westward.

Thousands were seeking that Zion in the Wilderness, leaving the older settlements along the Atlantic seaboard, and resettling in western New York, Ohio, Indiana, Kentucky and Tennessee. The combined ministerial forces of the Presbyterians and the Congregationalists were unable to keep up with this new challenge.

By 1843, Dr. Marcus Whitman, a physician and Presbyterian ruling elder, had led a thousand settlers over the Oregon Trail, spurred by a desire to bring the Indians of Oregon medical care and the Gospel. Those settlers faced enormous odds as they crossed the Rockies in covered wagons. Dr. and Mrs. Whitman themselves were murdered by Indians during a measles epidemic.

Yet these two Calvinistic communions experienced a rate of growth during this period which has never since been equalled. Between 1800-37, membership increased eleven-fold, jumping from 20,000 to 220,000 in the Presbyterian Church alone.

However, growing pains accompanied the swelling membership rolls. Again, the question of ministerial training arose as revivals in Kentucky and Tennessee, as well as elsewhere, made it impossible for the churches to supply enough pastors to minister to the new converts.

In an effort to meet the growing demands of the frontier, the Cumberland Presbytery petitioned the Synod of Kentucky to lower the educational standards for candidates for the ministry. However, the synod flatly rejected the overture, thereby bringing about the so-called "Cumberland Schism" and the establishment of the Cumberland Presbyterian Church in 1810.

It may appear that the main body of Presbyterians was particularly hard-nosed about this matter of education. However, the glory of the church since the days of John Calvin had been its educated ministry. Moreover, many were suspicious of the excesses of the frontier revivals, a phenomenon which had been absent during the earlier Great Awakening.

Not that the Presbyterian Church was oblivious to the need for more ministers. It was, in fact, during this period that many of the great Presbyterian seminaries were established. "In this way," says Benjamin J. Lake, "the church attempted to meet the need for well-trained men, a need that increased as each year went by."

Meanwhile, doctrinal differences had arisen between the Presbyterians and the Congregationalists. This led to a cleavage between the Old School and New School parties within the church, with the Old School holding a majority at the General Assembly of 1837. Says Walter Lingle:

> With this majority they passed a resolution which declared that the plan of the cooperative union with the Congregational Church in 1801, was unconstitutional from the beginning, and that all that was done under the plan was null and void. By this resolution four entire western synods that had been organized under this plan were cut off, root and branch. This split the Presbyterian Church almost . . . in two, and each half became a separate and distinct denomination of Presbyterians. The Old School Presbyterian Church had about 120,000 members, and the New School Presbyterian Church had about 100,000 members, about 10,000 of whom lived in the South. This division was a severe blow to Presbyterianism in America.

Adding to Presbyterian woes at this time were the gathering clouds of war, which would split the Baptist and Methodist churches over the question of slavery within the next few years. In 1857, the same prospect awaited the Presbyterians when the New School church divided at the Mason-Dixon Line.

Four years later, in May, 1861, the atmosphere was tense when the Old School General Assembly met in Philadelphia. The War Between the States had already begun, and few Southern commissioners had been able to travel north for the sessions.

This absence of full Southern participation in the deliberations made it possible for the General Assembly to adopt the so-called Gardiner Spring Resolutions, by a vote of 156 to 66.

These resolutions affirmed the General Assembly's decision, "in the spirit of Christian patriotism which the Scriptures enjoin and which has always characterized this church . . . (to) hereby acknowledge and declare our obligation to promote and perpetuate, so far as in us lies, the integrity of these United States, and to strengthen, uphold and encourage the Federal Government in the exercise of all its functions under our noble Constitution.

"To this Constitution, in all its provisions, requirements and principles," the resolutions added, "we profess our unabated loyalty."

But such "unabated loyalty" to the Federal Government and its Constitution was impossible for these Southern Presbyterians, who now lived in states which had seceded from the Union and now comprised the Confederate States of America!

The adoption of the Gardiner Spring Resolutions pointed up the paradox—the tension—which confronted Presbyterians ever since the days of Calvin and Knox. That tension revolved around the question of determining what belongs to Caesar and what belongs to God.

Presbyterians throughout Europe and in colonial America had repeatedly been on the side of the free exercise of religion and against the encroachments of the state. They had cheerfully been branded as heretics and traitors. And now the brethren in the North were asking 100,000 Presbyterians in the South to commit high treason against the government of the Confederate States of America.

In this instance, the Southerners took the position that the General Assembly had no authority to issue pronouncements demanding political compliance. It was a view shared by many thoughtful Presbyterians in the North, including the great theologian, Charles Hodge of Princeton Theological Seminary.

This controversy has dogged the steps of the Presbyterians, as well as members of other denominations, down to the present day. It is a controversy which involves one's understanding of the very nature and demands of the Gospel itself.

Some insist that the so-called social implications of the Gospel make it imperative for Christians to speak out on a wide variety of social, political and economic questions.

Others, including many Presbyterians in the South, contend just as forcefully that there must be changed men before there can be a changed society.

But all Presbyterians would agree that John Calvin himself was correct when he declared that "God alone is the Lord of the conscience."

Meanwhile, the Presbyterian Church—no less than the nation—was split by the cruel realities of the War Between the States. In 1837, there had been only one church. Now there were four: the New School North and the New School South, and the Old School North and the Old School South. Each comprised a separate and distinct denomination.

The breach between the two northern branches of the church was thankfully healed in 1870. But the Southern brethren rejected all overtures for reunion at the war's end.

The man who had unwittingly played a major role in the division was a Presbyterian by the name of Abraham Lincoln, regarded in the North as the "Great Emancipator," and in somewhat less affectionate terms in the South.

Catherine Marshall tells a delightful story which indicates that some Southerners still aren't prepared to forgive Mr. Lincoln.

It seems as though her distinguished husband, the late Reverend Dr. Peter Marshall, had an elderly friend from Marietta, Georgia, who sometimes worshiped at the New York Avenue Presbyterian Church, Washington, D.C., while he served as pastor there.

"Whenever that spirited unreconstructed rebel 'Miss Mary' visited us . . ." says Catherine Marshall, "as she passed the Lincoln pew, she always jocularly stuck out her tongue."

Rummaging through the trustees' records of the New York Avenue Church, Mrs. Marshall discovered that the

President had been behind in his pew rent at the time of his assassination.

But that didn't keep him from establishing a warm relationship with the pastor, the Reverend Phineas D. Gurley, who became a close friend and adviser to the Lincoln family.

While critics have sometimes claimed that Mr. Lincoln was "an open scoffer at Christianity," quite the opposite was true. He had an amazing grasp of the English Bible, whose hallowed words flavored so many of his speeches. But he also believed a man should live his faith.

On one occasion, says Catherine Marshall, "a forlorn, bedraggled-looking man came wandering down the center aisle looking for a seat. The President noticed him. Instantly, out shot a long arm, and (a) young couple heard the President whisper, 'Come right in beside me, brother, there's *plenty* of room . . .' "

Carl Sandburg tells another story which indicates that Abe Lincoln's compassion extended to former enemies. Senator Charles Sumner of Massachusetts had approached the President, says Mr. Sandburg, to insist that Confederate leader Jefferson Davis be hanged after the war. But Lincoln replied calmly: "Judge not, that ye be not judged."

"Again," says Sandburg, "as Sumner later wrote of it, he pressed Lincoln with a remark that the sight of Libby Prison made it impossible to pardon the President of the Confederate States, and Lincoln repeated twice over the words, 'Judge not, that ye be not judged.' "

At war's end, the major Presbyterian bodies began to move forward once again, rebuilding "the house divided against itself," and answering new challenges in the West. Abroad, Presbyterian missionaries moved into Korea, Japan and other nations which had not yet heard the Gospel of Christ.

But a war of a different sort was looming on the horizon. It was to cut across denominational lines as American churchmen became acquainted with the new "higher criticism" of the Bible, which was largely the product of German scholarship. In a word, more orthodox church leaders feared that such scholarship would undermine the authority of Scripture, "the only infallible rule for faith and practice."

Their fears were heightened by the publication of Charles Darwin's *Origin of Species* (1859), which appeared to undermine the Genesis account of creation. Some influential clergymen, such as Lyman Abbott, attempted to come to terms with evolution by accepting its major themes, while retaining their basic belief in God as the originator of the evolutionary process. Others rejected Darwin's findings out-of-hand.

Out of the revolutionary climate created by higher criticism and the new science came the heresy trial of the distinguished Hebrew scholar Charles A. Briggs, who was first brought to trial by New York Presbytery and later deposed from the Presbyterian ministry by the General Assembly of 1893. Another eminent scholar, A. C. McGiffert, withdrew from the Presbytery rather than face a similar ordeal.

This so-called Modernist-Fundamentalist controversy finally reached its climax during the 1930s, following a decision by conservative theologian John Gresham Machen to leave Princeton Seminary and establish a new school, Westminster, for the training of orthodox ministers. It appeared by this time that the Modernists had won.

However, other forces were also at work during this stormy period, as Presbyterian statesmen, such as Arthur Judson Brown and Robert E. Speer, were catching the glimpse of a church which transcended all denominational, racial and national boundaries. Their insights were to pave the way for the ecumenical movement. But that is another story.

6

What's in a Name?

HER MAJESTY the Queen may rule Britannia. But she does not rule the Church of Scotland!

The fiercely independent Scots will continue to drive home this point each year when the Queen's own representative shows up for the opening session of the General Assembly of the Scottish Kirk, the nearest thing to a Parliament Scotland has had for three centuries.

For the duration of the assembly, the Queen's representative holds the rank of Number Two man in the realm. His title is lord high commissioner. And he resides in the palace at Holyrood House, his flag flying above the heather and thistle.

"But for all his fancy titles," *The Chicago Tribune* once observed, "he comes to the assembly only as an observer, and, for the first few minutes, he will be completely ignored.

"The rudeness," explained *The Tribune*, "is calculated

to put him in his proper place as an uninvited guest."

For Jesus Christ alone is the Head of the Kirk of Scotland.

In actual practice, all human authority rests within the "priesthood of believers," "God's own elect." Commissioners to the assembly itself are teaching and ruling elders—a gamekeeper or clan chieftain from a Highland parish, a professor from New College in Edinburgh, a grocer from Dundee, an inner city pastor from Glasgow.

Clergy and laymen have equal voice in the deliberations of the assembly. Her Majesty's "lord high commissioner" has none.

Delegates may agree privately that the Queen's representative is a good enough chap. Any rudeness directed against him is merely symbolic. It is based upon a long-standing principle. It does not involve any personalities.

That principle goes back to those stormy days when Mary Queen of Scots sought to elevate the crown above the church. However, an unbending John Knox demanded complete independence for the kirk—and got it. Mary got only the right to send an observer to its assemblies.

Of course, there have been a few unfortunate occasions during which the "lord high commissioner" foolishly attempted to overstep his bounds. Such an event occurred in 1638, when the agent of the crown ordered the General Assembly to adjourn. But the meeting went on. King or no king.

No wonder, then, that James I wryly observed that "presbytery agreeth with monarchy like God and the devil."

Maybe Andrew Melville wasn't quite fair in dismissing James as "God's silly vassal." For he sure hit the nail on the head that time.

John Richard Green summed up the entire matter when he noted that the government of the Presbyterian Church was conceived of as "a Christian state in which the true sovereign was not pope or bishop (or king) but the Christian man."

American Presbyterians may not bring to their General Assemblies the pomp and circumstance of the Church of Scotland. But they're still a fiercely independent lot, shunning all outside interference and demanding equality in voice and vote for clergy and laity alike.

You won't find the word *presbyterian* in the Bible—unless you know a bit of Greek.

However, if you *are* familiar with the Greek New Testament, you will soon find almost countless references to the *presbyterios*. They were presbyters—or elders—who were selected to supervise the work of the church in far-flung cities across Asia Minor. Elders were entrusted with similar responsibilities in Old Testament Judaism.

The name Presbyterian therefore refers to a particular form of church government. All authority is entrusted under this system to the elders of the congregation (called the Session) and to the other courts of the church.

The Presbyterian forefathers adopted this distinctive type of polity because they thought it was the most Biblical and in keeping with New Testament Christianity. In doing so, they rejected two other forms of government still used by churches today.

One of those other systems is known as the *episcopal* form of government. The name comes from another Greek word, *episkopos,* which is variously translated as guardian, overseer, or bishop. In common usage, an *episcopal* church is one which is ruled by *bishops*. Those churches which have adopted an episcopal form of government include the Roman Catholic Church, the Anglican Church, the Protestant Episcopal Church, the United Methodist Church, and some of the Lutheran churches of Europe, Asia, and Africa.

The third system of church polity is known as the *congregational* form of government. In this system, the local *assembly* of believers is conceived as being independent in matters of order, discipline and action. It also furthers the notion that majority rule determines the course of action a given congregation will take in a specific matter. Churches with a congregational form of government include the Baptist bodies and the United Church of Christ.

Now let's look at the question of government a little deeper.

The Presbyterian forefathers, quite apart from the Bible, had some very strong objections to episcopacy. They had seen how corrupt bishops could become. They had also chafed under many decrees of various popes which they considered thoroughly unscriptural. Therefore, they wanted no part of any church in which one man—or any group of men—could lord it over other believers.

But they also had reservations about the congregational form of government. They considered such a system almost a form of religious anarchy. For they understood only too well that man, sinner that he is, could wreck the Church of Christ by allowing a strong personality to dominate a majority. There must be, they felt, an appellate system, a kind of court of last resort in which to bring grievances that threatened to split the local congregation.

So they searched the Scriptures and discovered that the Bible knew nothing of popes, prelates, monks, or abbots. It did, however, speak of apostles, prophets, evangelists, pastors and teachers. "Of these," said Calvin, "only the two last sustain an ordinary office in the church; the others were such as the Lord raised up at the commencement of His Kingdom, and such as He still raises up on particular occasions, when required by the necessity of the times."

For example, this "necessity of the times" might cause the Lord to raise up a George Whitefield, Dwight L. Moody, or Billy Graham to call a backsliding nation back to God. But He has left the ordinary ongoing work of His church to the pastors and teachers.

But the Bible also makes frequent use of the terms elder and deacon. In Acts 14: 23, for instance, we learn that Paul and Barnabas ordained elders in every church which they organized. We further find that Paul sent for the elders of the church at Ephesus to meet him at Miletus (Acts 20: 17). And, in Titus 1: 5, the apostle commanded Titus to ordain elders in every city. "These passages are sufficient to show," says Walter Lingle, "that the New Testament church was governed by elders."

In Old Testament usage, the term elder referred to a Hebrew word which meant "chin" or "beard." Thus, the elders of the congregation of Israel were expected to be men of full stature, who exercised maturity of judgment and the power of a "full-bearded" personality. These same qualifications were expected of the elder in the Church of Jesus Christ.

But there are five places in the New Testament in which the term bishop occurs. This would appear to be sufficient to knock the Presbyterian position into a cocked hat.

However, closer examination shows us, as Alan Richardson points out, that the words elder and bishop "appear to have been two names for the same office-bearers" in apostolic times. The notion of a bishop with the powers of a prelate is completely foreign to New Testament faith and life.

In Biblical usage, the word bishop is nontechnical and is used interchangeably with elder. For example, Paul speaks of the elders of the Ephesian Church in Acts 20: 17; yet eleven verses later, in Acts 20: 28, he refers to these same men as bishops, or as "overseers to feed the Church of God." This same fact can be seen by comparing Titus 1: 5 with Titus 1: 7.

Even the distinguished Bishop Joseph Barber Lightfoot and other Anglican scholars have conceded that elders and bishops are identical in the New Testament. They are simply different names for the same office.

However, the Presbyterian Church has claimed that the Bible gives support for the concept of both *teaching* and *ruling* elders. The pastor is meant to teach, while the laity is expected to rule. This means that the church can never be "priest-ridden" or "clergy dominated." For the real authority of the local church is vested in elect laymen who demonstrate Christian maturity and show the power of Christ in their lives.

Presbyterians look to I Timothy 5: 17 for Biblical support for their notion that Scripture allows two types of elders. In that passage, Paul tells his "own son in the faith" that "elders that rule well (should) be counted worthy of double honour, especially they who labour in the word and doctrine."

The Roman Catholic Church insists that Peter was the first pope. But, while there is some evidence that he held a unique place among the apostles, the Big Fisherman himself felt much more at home with the simple title of elder (I Peter 5: 1). He was merely a dedicated teaching elder, and he reserved for Jesus Christ alone the august title of "the Shepherd and Bishop of your souls" (I Peter 2: 25).

Moreover, there is strong New Testament support for the belief that elders in apostolic times were elected by the people themselves, and not by any ecclesiastical hierarchy. In Acts 14: 23, for example, we learn that elders were ordained in *every* church. A synod or annual conference had nothing to do with it.

Walter S. Lingle makes the interesting observation that the Greek word translated "ordain" in this passage literally means the raising of hands. "It may refer to the election of elders by the raising of hands," he says, "rather than to their ordination by the laying on of hands."

That this *representative* form of government continued

into the immediate post-apostolic era is suggested by a comment of Clement of Rome, writing about 100 A.D., that church officers were elected "by the consent of the whole people."

To this day, ruling elders of the Presbyterian Church are elected, ordained, and installed by the local congregation. In taking their vows, they accept the Scriptures as "the only infallible rule of faith and practice," and confess their faith in "the Lord Jesus Christ as . . . Savior and Lord." They further pledge "to study the peace, unity, and purity of the church."

In accepting their new officers, members of the congregation are required to "promise to yield to them all that honor, encouragement, and obedience in the Lord to which their office, according to the Word of God and the constitution of this church, entitles them." Then, after a brief prayer, the new ruling elders are ordained by the pastor with the words:

> *Set apart, O Lord, these thy servants, to the work whereunto they have been called by the voice of the church. Endue them plenteously with Heavenly wisdom. Grant them thy grace, that they may be good men, full of the Holy Spirit and of faith, ruling in the fear of God. Give them that favor and influence with the people which come from following Christ. So fill them with His Spirit that they may lead this congregation in His service. Make them faithful unto death, and when the Chief Shepherd shall appear, may they receive a crown of glory that fadeth not away. Amen.*

Meanwhile, the pastor or teaching elder, is *called* by the local congregation, but *ordained* and *installed* by the Presbytery *within the bounds* of which he has been called to serve. In his vows, he promises faithfulness to the Word of God, subjection to his brethren in the Lord, and to be an example of "piety before the flock over which God shall make (him) overseer."

It is a solemn moment for the young minister (and his

wife) when he kneels before the moderator and other members of Presbytery to be ordained to the Gospel ministry. As his fellow ministers—his "brethren in the Lord" —place their hands upon his head, the moderator prays:

Send down thy Holy Spirit upon this thy servant, whom we, in thy name and in obedience to the holy will, do now by the laying on of our hands ordain and appoint to the office of the holy ministry in thy church, committing unto him authority to preach the word, administer the sacraments, and to bear rule in thy church.

In accepting the call of a local congregation, the new pastor will promise to "promote the glory of God, and the good of His church," maintaining "a deportment in all respects becoming a minister of the Gospel of Christ."

In return, the members of the congregation will be called upon to pledge to their new pastor a receptive heart "to receive the Word of truth from his mouth, with meekness and love." They will further promise to "encourage him in his arduous labor," and to provide "competent worldly maintenance . . . and whatever else you may see needful for the honor of religion, and his comfort among you."

The powers of the minister are few but important. In addition to being responsible for the conduct of public worship, the pastor alone determines "whose children he will baptize, whom he will marry, and how he will fulfill his many responsibilities subject only to the Presbytery, and not to the rule of the ruling elders, much less the board of trustees or the congregation."

The teaching and ruling elders are *ordained for life.* But either can be suspended or deposed from their respective ministries for a serious violation of the Word of God or the constitution of the church.

Moreover, under the rotary system of the United Presbyterian Church, ruling elders are permitted to serve only two three-year terms as active members of the session. Then they must take at least a one-year break, which is designed to bring new people into the work of ministry and to insure against the possibility of a man or group of men lording it over their brethren in the Church of Christ. In the church of John Knox at Geneva, it will be recalled, the pastor and the elders and deacons were elected for only one year at a time to guard against this possibility.

While the authority of the local church is vested in the elders, the early church found that ministers of the Word were unable to meet the demands of an ever-growing number of converts to the Gospel. There were the poor and needy, the orphans and widows in their affliction, who required the compassionate hand of the compassionate Christ.

So the church at Jerusalem appointed "seven men of honest report, full of the Holy Ghost and wisdom" to assist the twelve apostles in their heavy work load (Acts 6: 1-8). One of those seven men was Stephen, the first martyr of the Cross.

Christian tradition has identified these men as deacons, a term which is found only in Philippians 1: 1 and I Timothy 3: 10-13. Their qualifications are described in the second passage, but nothing is said of their duties.

The story of the appointment of the seven in Acts does not use the word deacons; but it does use the Greek verb from which the term is derived. They were to be servants, fulfilling those works of charity required by the church, and relieving the apostles by relieving the poor.

Therefore, the Presbyterian churches still recognize the office of the deacon as a valid ministry required by the apostles themselves. In a lovely passage, *The Book of Common Worship* of the United Presbyterian Church contains these words for the ordination of deacons:

Beloved in Christ: In the Christian Churches of apostolic times there were deacons, whose office was held in honor, and who were highly esteemed for their services to the Church, in company with the elders. From early days it was a peculiar part of the duties of these office-bearers to be the instruments of the Church's ministry of compassion. This Church, therefore, has recognized the office and work of the deacons as in accord with apostolic practice. In the course of time new forms of work have been given to this office, and it has grown in value to the Church, while to it there has always attached its ancient character as the representative of the Church's purpose to follow Christ in compassion and in ministry to the bodily needs of men.

But, while the office has always been highly esteemed, the elders alone bear rule on the session, the governing body of the local church. The pastor, or teaching elder, serves as the moderator of this basic court in the Presbyterian structure. He is assisted by the *clerk of session* in making certain that all meetings are conducted "decently and in order."

In churches today, state law requires that certain adult members in every congregation be designated or elected to handle *corporate* business. This would involve such matters as church property and other concerns of a legal nature. Those who are delegated such responsibilities are called *trustees*. Therefore, many churches have three types of officers: elders, deacons, and trustees.

However, other congregations have adopted what is known as the *unicameral* system of government, under which both the spiritual and temporal concerns of the church are handled by a single board.

In actual practice, however, Presbyterian law requires that *every* congregation be governed under a unicameral system. For all authority ultimately resides in the session. It is the elders—and the elders alone—who *delegate* certain powers and responsibilities to the deacons and trustees. They further have the final word on the Sunday school and other organizations of the church.

But what happens if controversy threatens to disrupt the "peace, unity, and purity" of the local congregation? For trouble sometimes hits the best of churches.

This is the beauty of the Presbyterian form of government. It is a *connectional* church. The local congregation is never alone. It is tied to other believers through the presbytery, synods and General Assembly of the church.

These three larger bodies are called the higher courts or *judicatories* of the denomination. It might be said that the session serves as the local magistrate, the presbytery as the municipal court, the synod as the State Court of Appeals, and the General Assembly as the Supreme Court of the Presbyterian Church. When the General Assembly has spoken, there is no further court of appeals.

However, these four judicatories have other than a judicial function. For they are charged under the constitution to exercise executive and legislative authority as well. So it is that a distinguished jurist once remarked: "The framers of the Constitution of the United States borrowed very much of the form of our Republic from the Constitution of the Presbyterian Church of Scotland."

What he meant was that our colonial forefathers, in attempting to create a truly *representative* form of government, established three separate and distinct branches—executive, legislative and judicial—to act as a system of checks and balances against the possibility of one branch gaining control over the other two.

This does not mean that mistakes cannot sometimes be made. "All synods and councils since the apostles' times . . . may err, and many have erred," declares our Westminster Confession of Faith. "Therefore they are not to be made the rule of faith or practice, but to be used as a help in both."

The local churches of a particular geographical area are specifically united to the Presbytery, which consists of all the ministers and one ruling elder from each congregation in that area. In a very real sense, the presbytery is the basic unit of the Presbyterian form of government.

The constitution of the Presbyterian Church has entrusted to the presbytery a host of wide-ranging powers. Among them are the powers to examine and ordain candidates to the Gospel ministry, condemn erroneous opinions hurtful to the life of the church, review the records of all sessions annually, and to exercise ultimate control over all church property within its bounds.

The structures of the church may change with the changing times. For example, Presbyterians North and South have recently been at work streamlining the boards and agencies and creating regional synods to replace those established earlier along state lines. But the basic integrity of the Presbyterian form of government remains intact.

In all of the judicatories, the parity or equality of clergy and laity remains the glory of a noble heritage. At the local level, the session is composed of ruling elders, all of whom are laymen. The minister sits as moderator to conduct meetings; but it is the laymen who rule.

"Apart from the ruling elders, the pastor has very little authority of his own in a Presbyterian church," says the Reverend Dr. Eugene Carson Blake, former Stated Clerk of the United Presbyterian General Assembly and an authority on Presbyterian law. "Apart from the pastor . . . the ruling elders have practically no authority as a group or as individuals.

"A basic principle of Presbyterian government," he says, "is that authority is lodged in ordered groups and not in individuals."

It is important to remember that, while members of the congregation are subject to the discipline of the session, the minister is subject to the discipline of his "brethren in the Lord" in the presbytery. He is a member of the presbytery within whose bounds he labors; he is not a member of the congregation to which he has been called.

In the higher courts, there is absolute parity in the division of ministers and laymen. At the presbytery level, each congregation is directed to send the pastor and one ruling elder to all stated meetings. The presbyteries, in turn, elect an equal number of pastors and laymen to represent them at assemblies of the synods and the General Assembly.

But why can't the local congregation carry on its business—and fight its fights—without outside interference? Is there any Scriptural authority for this kind of church government?

While scholars have debated endlessly on this question, Paul admonishes Timothy not to neglect "the gift that is in thee, which was given thee by prophecy, with the laying on of the hands of the presbytery" (I Timothy 4: 14).

Here the actual word presbytery is used in the New Testament to refer to a council of representatives from the various churches, who were specifically charged with the solemn task of commissioning and ordaining new ministers for the work of the Gospel. It is used elsewhere (Luke 22: 66; Acts 22: 5) in reference to the Jewish Sanhedrin.

After examining all of the New Testament evidence, Alan Richardson has concluded: "In view of our uncertainty in the whole matter, *we can infer nothing from these passages except that ordination by a council of presbyters was known in the subapostolic church* and that it was believed that St. Paul ordained by the laying on of hands."

"Since the days of the first apostles," says this noted Bible scholar, "there have been no presbyters (or presbyter-bishops) who have not been ordained by the commissioning of the presbytery in the sense of I Timothy 4: 14.

"To claim that one has received a commission to minister directly from Christ Himself without the (authority)

84

of the appropriate organ of His Body the Church," says Dr. Richardson, "is to claim to be an apostle, to be another St. Paul. It is, in fact, to proclaim 'another gospel.' "

William Barclay makes the same point, insisting that the early church knew nothing of isolated or anonymous Christians and independent congregations. "The Christian leader does not make sense apart from the church," he writes. "His commission came from the church; his work is within the fellowship of the church; his duty is to build others into the church."

So many petty squabbles and serious divisions within the Body of Christ could be settled agreeably if only local congregations would heed the example of the apostles themselves and seek guidance from their "brethren in the Lord" in the presbytery.

There was the time, for example, when the church at Antioch was faced with the thorny question of whether a Gentile believer must first subscribe to all of the ordinances of Judaism before he could be admitted to membership in the church (Acts 15). Even Paul and Peter were in sharp disagreement on the matter.

"If the church at Antioch had been entirely independent it could have settled that question for itself," observes Walter Lingle. "With such leaders as Paul and Barnabas the church at Antioch was abundantly able to settle that question and any others that might arise.

"Instead of doing that," he says, "the church at Antioch referred the question to a church council which met in Jerusalem . . . Note well that the council was composed of apostles and elders. It must have looked a good deal like a Presbyterian synod or General Assembly.

"Note also that this council, composed of apostles and elders, after full deliberation settled the question *authoritatively* and the church at Antioch and all the other churches accepted its decision," he notes. "There was a tie that bound these New Testament churches together into one church."

Since the Reformation, other churches outside the Presbyterian and Reformed tradition have recognized the wisdom of this great New Testament principle. And, says a distinguished Irish scholar, "it is a simple historical fact of deep significance that, wherever it was permitted to shape itself spontaneously after Scripture, and without external interference, it assumed a Presbyterian form."

7

Let God Be God!

CATECHISM WAS SERVED with the porridge each morning
in the boyhood home of Thomas Carlyle in Dumfriesshire,
Scotland.

The day would come when Carlyle would be reckoned
among the literary giants of nineteenth-century Europe.
But he was never to forget those lessons learned at the
breakfast table over a bowl of piping hot cereal.

His mature years had been spent alternately criticizing
the weaknesses of democracy and championing the dignity of the common man. He had often used bombast to
expose the evils of industrial society and to offer his solu-
tions for correcting social inequities. Yet boyhood memories continued to dominate his thinking as he lashed out
at the faith of the materialist:

> The older I grow—and I now stand upon the brink
> of eternity—the more comes back to me the first
> sentence in the Catechism which I learned when a

child, and the fuller and deeper its meaning becomes: "What is the chief end of man? To glorify God and enjoy Him forever."

It is of course possible to dismiss the mellowed thinking of Thomas Carlyle as that of an old man awaiting death, a man grasping at straws as the Grim Reaper was beckoning from the wings.

But better to have the sovereign God of an intellectual giant than the puny gods of so many spiritual pygmies today. "Start with a little god and we have a little religion, inadequate to human needs," says Egbert Watson Smith. "A great religion demands a great God . . ."

"The root principle of Calvinism is the confession of God's absolute sovereignty," says Dr. Smith. "Not one special attribute of God, His love or justice, His holiness or equity, but God Himself *as such* . . . is the point of departure for the thinking and acting of the Calvinist.

"The *glory* of the Lord God Almighty is its unifying, all-pervading aim," he says. "Not bare sovereignty, arbitrary will, naked power, but a *personal* God of grace, the God *revealed in Christ,* is the God of Calvinism."

"In all places, in all time," someone has written, "from eternity to eternity, Calvinism sees God."

But is all of this just a pious and empty dream? Are Christians called upon to be something like the White Queen in Lewis Carroll's delightful fantasy, *Through the Looking Glass?*

"Now I'll give you something to believe," said the Queen. "I'm a hundred and one, five months and a day."

"I can't believe that," said Alice.

"Can't you?" the Queen said in a pitying tone. "Try again; draw a long breath, and shut your eyes."

Alice laughed. "There's no use trying," she said. "One can't believe impossible things."

"I dare say you haven't had much practice," said the Queen. "When I was your age, I always did it for half an

88

hour a day. Why, sometimes I've believed as many as six impossible things before breakfast."

Does Christianity likewise expect us to just close our eyes and believe a lot of "impossible things"? Like the existence of a God who not only cares but calls *you* by name?

There's an old Yiddish saying that a *phudnik* is a *nudnik* with a Ph.D. But the philosophers who have grappled with the question of God's existence were anything but *nudniks* when they laid down some pretty strong arguments for personal belief in deity. You might get the idea, however, that they were a bunch of *phudniks*—or at least pretty square—for using the inexpressible to describe the inexpressible. Words like cosmological, teleological and ontological!

What is a body to believe?

Actually, the *cosmological* argument makes pretty good sense. It simply says that behind every *effect* there must be an adequate *cause*. It has therefore sometimes been called the argument of causality.

Nobody in his right mind would dare to suggest that you could turn on your favorite tv program unless Consolidated Edison or Pacific Power & Gas provided the necessary electrical power. The program itself is only an effect. The electrical current is the cause that makes the program possible.

You'd probably call for a "shrink" if someone denied this proposition simply because he couldn't *see* the power of electricity at work. But the atheist is caught in this very trap when he denies the existence of a creator (the cause) behind the creation (the effect).

"The probability of life originating from accident," said biologist Edwin Conklin, "is comparable to the probability of the Unabridged Dictionary resulting from an explosion in a printing shop."

Or to put it another way, try this experiment suggested

by the onetime president of the New York Scientific Society:

Take ten identical coins and mark them one to ten. There is one chance in ten that you will get number one. Now replace it, and the chances that number two will follow number one are not one in ten, but one in one hundred. With each new coin taken out, the risk will be multiplied by ten, so that the chance of all ten following in sequence is one chance in 10,000,000,000 (ten billion).

That is why American statistician George Gallup has remarked: "I could prove God statistically. Take the human body alone—the chance that all the functions of the individual would just happen is a statistical monstrosity!"

"All right," you say, "if God made us, who made God?"

Tilt!

That question is out-of-bounds the minute you admit to the possibility of what Aristotle called the Causeless First Cause.

For once you concede the *possibility* of Deity, you run smack into the *ontological* argument of St. Anselm, a twelfth-century Archbishop of Canterbury, who, like a lot of modern Christians, was deeply troubled by the charge that God was only the figment of a pious imagination.

What Anselm came to realize was simply this: God is that than which nothing greater can be conceived.

If the God who created us was Himself created, that would mean that there was "a bigger and better god" beyond our wildest imaginations. We could just keep on going endlessly backward into the mystery of the divine, as indeed the Gnostics attempted to do, in our search for the sovereign God above all other gods.

But that is impossible to do once you accept Anselm's definition of deity. God is the epitome of absolute perfection. He is greater than that which can be conceived.

We can use the social analogy and say that God is to

us as a superior and benevolent human being is to other human beings. Or we can employ the mind-body analogy and suggest that God is the soul of the universe as the *real person* is the soul within the body. Or we can still use yet another analogy—the artistic analogy—and claim that God creatively produces and shapes the universe as the artist shapes a piece of clay.

Anselm's so-called "proof" for the existence of God finds added weight in the *teleological* argument. God is more than the Causeless First Cause. He is rather also what Plato called the Supreme Architect, a being with *intelligence* and *will,* not just a blind force.

If the poems and paintings of men demonstrate the reality of reason, then an orderly universe, governed by the times and the seasons, must give evidence of a rational character behind creation itself. There must be a designer behind the design.

"For myself," declared Nobel Prize winner Arthur Compton, "faith begins with a realization that a supreme intelligence brought the universe into being and created man. It is not difficult for me to have this faith, for it is incontrovertible that where there is a plan there is intelligence—an orderly, unfolding universe testifies to the truth of the most majestic statement ever uttered—'In the beginning God.' "

What would happen to any man foolish enough to claim that the Empire State Building was erected without the aid of an architect? Or that the intricate mechanism of a watch "just got there" without the design of a watchmaker? Yet the atheist would have us believe that genetic chain and the intricate workings of a well-functioning body "just got there" without the guidance of that supreme intelligence we Christians call God.

No wonder, then, that the psalmist declared: "The fool hath said in his heart, There is no God" (Psalm 14: 1).

But there is yet another argument for God's existence.

It is called the *moral* argument and was first suggested by the great German philosopher Immanuel Kant (1724-1804).

While Kant saw the weaknesses of the classical arguments for God, he was personally impressed by that sense of "oughtness" which seems to be built into the human personality. There are certain things that man instinctively knows he "ought" and "ought not" to do. "Were it not for the voice speaking so clearly in my conscience and my heart," said Cardinal John Henry Newman, "I should be an atheist, or a pantheist, when I looked into the world."

The Reverend Dr. Charles J. Woodbridge, a professor at Fuller Theological Seminary, used to tell the story of an encounter between a missionary and an African tribesman. "Tell me," asked the missionary, "do you believe in God?"

The African shook his head. "No."

"Do you sometimes do wrong?"

"Yes."

"Well," asked the missionary, "how do you know?"

"Because," replied the tribesman, "a little man inside my heart tells me so."

That's it. That's the *moral* argument.

Both young people and adults may sometimes live as though God just didn't exist. But in the solitude of their own souls they know perfectly well what the psalmist meant when he mused. "Whither shall I go from thy spirit? or whither shall I flee from thy presence? If I ascend up into heaven, thou art there: if I make my bed in hell, behold, thou art there" (Psalm 139: 7, 8).

But there's another side to the *moral* argument.

It is one thing to live in a world created by a great designer, a world fashioned by a Causeless First Cause. But that world would be a mockery and its creator a menace if injustice was always to be rewarded and justice ultimately defeated.

The very fact that the Stalins and Hitlers of world history have always met a just end testifies to the hope that the Judge of all men will one day settle the unsettled accounts of those who have brought madness and havoc into a weeping and despairing world.

There are some who have been naive enough to suggest that even the tyrant will find life in the world to come. But the orthodox Christian position has been expressed by James Russell Lowell:

> Though the cause of evil prosper,
>   Yet 'tis truth alone is strong;
> Truth forever on the scaffold,
>   Wrong forever on the throne,
> Yet that scaffold sways the future,
>   And, behind the dim unknown,
> Standeth God within the shadow
>   Keeping watch above His own.

Yet, having said all this, there are some pretty serious weaknesses concerning all of these arguments for the existence of God. It's not very comforting to think, for example, that your life is being guided by some great impersonal Causeless First Cause. Nor is it a comforting doctrine to discover that the great designer has apparently goofed. What purpose could there possibly be in the birth of a retarded or malformed child? Or in the "earthquake, wind, and fire" that kill thousands each year?

There is a certain disorder in an otherwise orderly universe which sometimes makes the most thoughtful person reassess the significance of the so-called *teleological* argument. In the face of such disorder, some find it impossible to echo the words of St. Paul: "O the depth of the riches both of the wisdom and knowledge of God! how unsearchable are his judgments, and his ways past finding out!" (Romans 11: 33).

Moreover, Immanuel Kant rejected Anselm's notion that God is that than which no greater can be conceived because, he suggested, the idea of $100 is not the same as having them in one's pocket.

But Kant's own *moral* argument has also had its share of critics. This so-called proof from practical reason rests upon the demands of man's moral nature. Conscience assumes that moral ideals can be realized; but they can be realized only if there is a supreme moral will. Morality inevitably leads to religion; and religion leads ultimately to God.

However, Immanuel Kant was writing before the revolution in anthropology and psychology. It is now questionable, say the critics, whether Kant would be as confident in submitting this "proof" in light of research which indicates that man's conduct is motivated by many unconscious urges and forces, while his conscience is largely determined by social and cultural factors. It is one thing to burp after a good meal in America, they say, and quite another in some other cultures! (Harvard Psychologist Gordon Allport has come to the service of the theologian by pointing out that the *content* of the conscience in no way does away with the conscience itself.)

At the same time, while there may be no atheists in foxholes, many boys have returned home from war with a deep conviction that a good God could never permit such bloodshed. They roundly reject Abraham Lincoln's notion that the hand of God may be at work even in the midst of this kind of senseless slaughter:

> Fondly do we hope—fervently do we pray—that this mighty scourge of war may speedily pass away. Yet, if God wills that it continue until all the wealth piled by the bondsman's two hundred and fifty years of unrequited toil shall be sunk, and until every drop of blood drawn with the lash shall be paid by another drawn with the sword, as was said three thousand years ago, so still it must be said, "The judgments of the Lord are true and righteous altogether."

That is where the debate surrounding the arguments for God's existence must be joined. None of these so-called proofs will appeal to the man who comes to God in doubt rather than in faith. Abraham Lincoln could only see the hand of God in the midst of war's confusion because he first accepted the words of the psalmist (19: 9)—and the Bible itself—as the revealed Word and will of God.

The question of whether God does or does not exist is not like a mathematical problem that can be solved without affecting our personal lives. "Religion is a most embarrassing subject," says Daniel Jenkins. "Nowhere is it more difficult for men to be honest than when they are approaching religion.

"Nothing is easier than to imagine that one is seeking . . . truth, when all that one is doing is either seeking ready confirmation of a faith one is too timid or lazy to scrutinize, or looking for a justification to continue in uncritical disbelief.

"To imagine that our own reasons are the only reliable courts of appeal in trying to discover grounds for belief in God," says Dr. Jenkins, "covers up the fundamental difficulty, which is that *we are not disinterested persons in this matter.*"

So many people simply refuse to accept the testimony of reason because deep within their heart of hearts they know that to believe in God is to obey and serve Him. For them, faith is not so much an intellectual problem as it is a moral problem. In a word, faced by the false glitter and glamor of the world, they are not yet prepared to say with Christ, "not my will, but thine, be done" (Luke 22: 42).

It was at this point that Calvin and the other Reformers differed sharply with the Scholastic theologians of the Roman Catholic Church. While St. Thomas Aquinas claimed that man could be led closer to God by the light of reason, Calvin insisted that man's *natural knowledge* of deity could only lead him to erect an *idol*. For Luther, it could only make him cringe before a knowledge of the *wrath* of God against all sin and disobedience.

This does not mean that Calvin denied the reality of that sense of the divine (the *sensus divinitatis*) in the most sinful of men. He himself readily conceded that, while the cruel Roman emperor Caligula "broke into (an) unbridled and audacicus contempt of the deity," none was ever more fearful of His wrath.

But, asks Calvin, of what value was that to him?

The most barbarous men and nations can apprehend some reality of deity from God's work in creation and preservation. Indeed, says Calvin, God Himself has implanted this "natural instinct" within man to prevent him from pretending ignorance of His existence.

Moreover, he writes, this natural instinct condemns man's own conscience whenever he forsakes the true God to worship the false gods of his own making. But some men still insist upon rejecting the God of the Bible to bow down before idols of wood and stone.

"Properly speaking," says Calvin, "we cannot say that God is known where there is no religion or piety . . .

"Cold and frivolous are the speculations of those who employ themselves in (questions) on the essence of God," he writes, "when it would be more interesting to us to become acquainted with His character, and to know what is agreeable to His nature . . ."

Then Calvin raises a question which is crucial for those who bandy about arguments for and against the existence of God. "What benefit arises," he asks, "from the knowledge of a God with whom we have no concern . . .?"

That's really getting down to basics. Right down to the nitty-gritty.

People so often do one of two things when it comes to "this God business." They either gamble that He doesn't exist. Or they "play" with Him as they would an idol of their own creation.

The first group includes those who live by the philosophy of eating, drinking and "living it up." They figure that time is short, too short to be bound by the mandates of the Almighty. And so, at best, they take their seats in the grandstand and make Christianity a spectator sport.

But every so often that natural instinct of which Calvin speaks comes into their thoughts to haunt them. Therefore, they resort to that age-old ruse of debating the "essence" of God in an almost last-ditch effort to quiet an uneasy conscience and to avoid any *personal encounter* with Him who demands that worship be more than an extracurricular activity.

But the second group is no better off. They seek to create God after their own image, and in their own likeness. He may be a projection of their own personalities. Or He may be no more than a parental hangover, a local policeman, the Grand Old Man, the Managing Director, the Pale Galilean, or simply The Man Upstairs.

If this is the kind of God *you* worship, says J. B. Phillips, then "your God is too small."

The gods of man's own making are sure to let him down in the crunch. They will no more be able to help a man through the "dark night of the soul" than the idols of ancient and modern paganism.

A great need demands a great God. The sexually-aroused teenager needs more than a god or goddess wrapped in *Playboy*. The shaking, sweating alcoholic needs more than a god-in-a-bottle. The "poor little rich kid" needs more than a bank account. And the scared young man in a foxhole needs more than a rifle.

So many people have put their trust in these "gods of the world," only to find that they have failed them in the moment of deepest need. Then they say ever afterwards, "We tried God once, but it didn't work. If there was a God, He wouldn't let us down."

But, in reality, the god these people followed was a god of their own making.

It is against this background of human idolatry that Calvinism declares: "Let God be God!"

The sovereign God of the Gospel can help the teenager overcome temptation, the alcoholic overcome his addiction, the "poor little rich kid" overcome an empty materialism, and a soldier his fright. He can even meet the needs of the orphan and the widow in their loneliness and affliction.

But this sovereign God is not found by man's unaided reason. He is, as Karl Barth said, the Wholly Other. And He reveals Himself in His Word and supremely in the life, death and resurrection of His only begotten Son.

"There is but one living and true God," declares *The Westminster Confession of Faith,* "who is infinite in being and perfection, a most pure spirit, invisible, without body, parts, or passions, immutable, immense, eternal, incomprehensible, almighty, most wise, most holy, most free, most absolute, working all things according to the counsel of His own immutable and most righteous will, for His own glory.

"But this God," assures the *Confession,* is also "most loving, gracious, merciful, long-suffering, abundant in goodness and truth, forgiving iniquity, transgression, and sin."

Best of all, assures the *Confession,* God is "the rewarder of them that diligently seek Him."

But, again, man's "natural knowledge" of God will only lead him to erect an idol or shudder before His wrath. His saving grace is found where He Himself is to be found. And that is within the sacred pages of the Holy Bible.

8

God Hath Spoken!

JOHN CALVIN was born to be a writer.

One biographer goes so far as to suggest that the Christian world would have had many more offerings from his prolific pen were it not for the fact that he had to waste so much of his time worrying about such petty matters as the clogged drains of Geneva—and its cantankerous politicians and churchmen.

Whatever the case, Calvin was a man of many words. But he was an author who used few illustrations. To him, literary ornamentation was as much to be avoided as man's "vain speculations" about God.

Therefore, when Calvin does use an illustration, it is to be taken all the more seriously.

T. H. L. Parker has pointed out that two literary images appear with regularity throughout the writings of the Master of Geneva. The first is *labyrinth,* while the second is the *Schoolmaster.*

Both of these images, says Dr. Parker, bear heavily upon Calvin's understanding of our knowledge of God and the authority of His Word.

In the opening words of *The Institutes of the Christian Religion,* Calvin had claimed that "true and substantial wisdom" involves "the knowledge of God, and the knowledge of ourselves."

But, he says, this all-important knowledge is corrupted as man finds himself in the midst of a labyrinth. He discovers that he is lost in a maze. He may possess "some sense of deity" through "natural instinct." But this instinct is obscured by *ignorance* and *wickedness.* Hence, says Calvin, men "worship not God but a figment of their own brains instead."

The more man seeks by his own unaided reason to understand the nature of God, he declares, the more he becomes lost in this labyrinth—a maze fashioned by the "inventions of (his) own presumptuous imaginations."

In fact, says Calvin, man can never come to a perfect knowledge of his great Creator-Redeemer unless God Himself breaks through the iron curtain man has erected around his idols—power, prestige, pleasure, success, science, and, most of all, the sacred cow of human reason.

Calvin saw clearly that man can never escape from the trap until he has corrected vision. And it is to the Scriptures that he must turn, he says, if he is to find the "glasses" needed to correct his spiritual blindness.

"It was necessary, in passing from death to life, that they should know God, not only as a Creator, but as a Redeemer also," he declares. "And both kinds of knowledge they certainly did obtain from the Word."

No man can have the least knowledge of God, he insists, until he becomes a reverent student of Scripture.

At the same time, Calvin recognized that the skeptic would never believe that the Bible contains the "spectacles" necessary for 20/20 spiritual vision. The only way many could be moved to accept the testimony of Scripture, he suggests, is through an authoritative testimony apart from the written Word itself.

But Calvin roundly rejected the "most pernicious error" that the authority of the Bible rests solely upon the testimony of the church. That would mean, he says, that "the eternal . . . truth of God depended on the arbitrary will of men."

"How will the impious ridicule our faith, and all men call it in question," he observes, "if it be understood to possess only a precarious authority depending on the favor of men."

Calvin scores some theological brownie points by making the shrewd observation that the church itself would never have been founded unless "the writings of the prophets and the preaching of the apostles" existed beforehand.

Some authority other than an often-corrupted and corrupting church is necessary, says Calvin, if the elect are to be led into a saving knowledge of God through the Scriptures.

"Our faith in doctrine is not established until we have a perfect conviction that God is its author," he declares. "Hence, the highest proof of Scripture is uniformly taken from the character of Him whose Word it is."

In a word, says Calvin, none other than the Holy Spirit Himself testifies within the hearts of God's elect that the Bible indeed is the trustworthy and authoritative Word of God.

"The prophets and apostles boast not of their own genius, or any of those talents which (inspire) the faith of the hearers," he observes. "Nor do they insist on arguments from reason, but bring forward the sacred Name of God to compel the submission of the whole world."

Since God alone "is a sufficient witness of Himself in His own Word," says Calvin, it is nothing other than "great folly" to attempt to demonstrate to "infidels" the authority and inspiration of Holy Scripture. This authority and inspiration, he insists, "cannot be known without faith."

However, the authority of the Word is self-evident to all who have received this gift of faith. "The Holy Spirit is . . . like a guarantee which confirms in our hearts the certainty of the divine truth . . ." says Calvin. "The Spirit itself beareth witness with our spirit, that we are the children of God" (Romans 8: 16).

"One must not imagine that the Christian faith is a bare and mere knowledge of God or an understanding of the Scripture which flutters in the brain without touching the heart . . ." he writes. "But faith is a firm and solid confidence of the heart, by means of which we rest surely in the mercy of God which is promised to us through the Gospel."

That is what separates the most humble and unlettered believer from the most educated, yet unbelieving, scholar.

The skeptic is like the man who has an appointment to meet a friend at Times Square but shows up at Greenwich Village instead. He has the wrong address, and, search though he will, he will never be able to locate his friend in the maze of the Village streets.

Similarly, man has a divine appointment with his Maker. God has given us an address and told us where to meet Him. That "address" is the Bible. And it will do us no good whatever to search out this Friend—this waiting Father—in the Greenwich Village of creation or conscience, or in the course of human history and experience.

To rely on such speculations, says Calvin, is like picking up the wrong street map. They can only lead us deeper into the maze—the labyrinth—of our minds' own making.

"There is nothing Calvin dislikes more than speculation," says Dr. Parker. "Speculation is man's bypassing the Scriptures so as to arrive at some idea of his own about God; and it is also a going beyond Scripture, so as to inquire into mysteries on which the Bible is silent."

Those who dig their spiritual forks deep into the sturdy meat-and-potatoes theology of Calvin are sure of two things: They will forever be freed from the bondage of skepticism and the bondage of the cults. More important, they will possess a *saving* knowledge of God and be able to give a ready answer to all men regarding the hope that lies within them (I Peter 3: 15).

However, John Calvin also used the figure of the *Schoolmaster* to demonstrate man's relationship to God and God's relationship to the Bible. God is *the* schoolmaster, he suggests. The school or lessons are the Scriptures. And man is the pupil.

God is first of all the schoolmaster in the sense that He Himself provided the Textbook necessary for a saving knowledge of His mighty works in creation and redemption. All of the writings of Scripture owe their origin to God alone.

"God has spoken, and, inspired by Him, men have passed on His Word in writing," says Dr. Parker. "For all its human quality, the Bible is not only the 'word' of its human writers but the Word of its Divine inspirer.

"So," he adds, "in the Scriptures God teaches us about Himself, about ourselves and about the world we live in. In this way He is our schoolmaster."

However, this does not mean that the Bible should be used as a textbook on science, philosophy or history. God's Word is truth. But that truth is meant primarily for our edification—and not a secular education.

At the same time, Calvin would insist that much that goes under the guise of knowledge is nothing more than a passing fad or vain speculation. St. Paul summed up the matter when he wrote: "If any man teach otherwise, and consent not to wholesome words, even the words of our

Lord Jesus Christ, and to the doctrine which is according to godliness; He is proud, knowing nothing . . ." (I Timothy 6: 3, 4a).

"But plain as the Scriptures are," says Parker, "the blindness of our understanding is such that they are above our comprehension. If we were left to ourselves in trying to understand and profit from this Book, we should fail totally."

Our problem with the Bible is not unlike that of the American teenager when he is first introduced to ninth-grade Latin. It all looks like Greek.

So God becomes our schoolmaster in yet another way. He interprets the language of Heaven in terms which can be understood in the human heart. Or, as the hymnwriter put it:

> God is His own interpreter,
> And He will make it plain.

Unless the Holy Spirit acts as our schoolmaster in this sense, the Bible will always remain a dull and lifeless Book. "For my thoughts are not your thoughts, neither are your ways my ways, saith the Lord. For as the heavens are higher than the earth, so are my ways higher than your ways, and my thoughts than your thoughts" (Isaiah 55: 8, 9).

Calvin readily accepts the notion that you can tell a man's school by his character. If the man is a good student, he says, "and his master is a good teacher too, he will certainly not only remember what he has been taught, but will also retain some characteristic of his master, so that it will be said, 'He was at such and such a school.' "

And that, says Calvin, is precisely the way it is with those who have sat at the feet of the Divine Schoolmaster.

One of the marks of God's elect is that they demonstrate humble submission to the voice of the Holy Spirit in the Word of God. For the Lord Jesus Himself assured: "I am the good shepherd, and know my sheep, and am known of mine. My sheep hear my voice, and I know them, and they follow me" (John 10: 14, 27).

Therefore, even the Old Testament psalmist could rejoice in the truth: "The law of the Lord is perfect, converting the soul . . . The statutes of the Lord are right, rejoicing the heart: the commandment of the Lord is pure, enlightening the eyes" (Psalm 19: 7, 8).

This was the faith of John Calvin. He built an entire theology around the conviction that "the prophecy came not in old time by the will of man: but holy men of God spake as they were moved by the Holy Ghost" (II Peter 1: 21). Therefore, "all scripture is given by inspiration of God, and is profitable for doctrine, for reproof, for correction, for instruction in righteousness: That the man of God may be perfect, throughly furnished unto all good works" (II Timothy 3: 16, 17).

A man will search in vain for human speculation within *The Institutes of the Christian Religion* or any other of Calvin's writings. "The only judgment that he would recognize as valid is the judgment of the Scriptures," says Parker. "We miss the mark if we judge his theology by any other standard.

"It stands or falls," he writes, "according to its faithfulness to the Word of God."

It is not surprising, therefore, to find that Calvin brought his high regard for the Bible into the pulpit with him. "When we enter the pulpit," he declared, "it is not so that we may bring our own dreams and fancies with us."

Calvin knew nothing of topical preaching. He rather took a single book, and then faithfully interpreted the text verse-by-verse. When he was through, he started expounding another book.

And the famous *Ordinances of the Church in Geneva* clearly demonstrate that what Calvin did from the pulpit of St. Peter's, he expected other pastors to do as well. The doctors of the church were admonished by the *Ordinances* "to instruct believers in wholesome doctrine, so that the purity of the Gospel shall not be adulterated by ignorance or false opinions."

But that does not mean that Calvin was a dry and "irrelevant" preacher. He constantly sought to translate the words of the ancient text into language which would meet the needs and concerns of his sixteenth-century listeners. Moreover, there were times when Calvin even felt duty bound to admonish his congregation to get out and vote. And vote for God-fearing men!

"When we are going to elect men to some public position, we must set about it reverently and carefully," he declared in one sermon. "For we shall provoke God's anger if we pollute the seat of justice, putting men in it who have neither the zeal nor the interest to honor and serve it."

However, Calvin's primary goal was to build Christians in the faith "once delivered unto the saints." In a sermon on I Timothy 6: 12-14, for example, he pointed out that the Christian life is one of constant struggle.

"St. Paul has declared . . . that we must fight . . . that faith cannot exist without conflict," Calvin observed. "Whoever wants his service to be approved by God, must get ready for battle. For we have an enemy who never slackens . . .

"Even if a Christian man did not go outside himself," he declared, "he would still need to fight to persist in the faith. For it is a fact that there is nothing more contrary to our nature than to leave earthly things and not be devoted to them . . .

"A Christian man," he admonished, "must rise above himself when it is a question of thinking of the Kingdom of God and everlasting life . . ."

So popular were Calvin's sermons that a group of French immigrants to Geneva hired a poor man by the name of Denis Raguenier to take down every word in shorthand. Raguenier did his job well—and it is thanks to him that we still possess more than a thousand sermons preached from the pulpit of St. Peter's by the indomitable Master of Geneva.

Where the wheezing, asthmatic Calvin left off in his preaching, men like John Knox and Francis Makemie took over. For all who came under his influence in Geneva perpetuated his commitment to the Word of God.

Even a quick study of the creeds of the Presbyterian and Reformed Faith shows that all were built on the premise that the Bible—and the Bible alone—is "the only infallible rule for faith and practice." These creeds further show that the Protestant Reformation of the sixteenth-century was essentially a back-to-the-Bible movement. Its watchword was this: *Sola gratia! Sola fide! Sola Scriptura!* Grace only! Faith only! Scripture only!

For example, the *Second Helvetic Confession,* one of the most widely used creeds of the Reformed churches, sharply condemns interpreting Scripture by the light of church councils, human tradition, and the opinions of men "adorned with high-sounding titles." It further rejects any notion that God has any other Word for sinful, despairing mankind outside the pages of the Bible.

Similarly, the great *Scots Confession* supports Calvin's insistence that the authority of Scripture is entirely independent from any authority of the church:

> We affirm, therefore, that those who say the Scriptures have no other authority save that which they have received from the Kirk are blasphemous against God and injurious to the true Kirk, which always hears and obeys the voice of her own Spouse and Pastor, but takes not upon her to be mistress over the same.

"The authority of the Holy Scripture, for which it ought to be believed and obeyed," declares the *Westminster Confession of Faith,* "dependeth not upon the testimony of any man or church, but wholly upon God (who is truth itself), the author thereof; and therefore it is to be received because it is the Word of God.

"The infallible rule of *interpretation* of Scripture is the Scripture itself," says the *Westminster Confession*. "Therefore, when there is a question about the true and full sense of any Scripture . . . it may be searched and known by other places that speak more clearly."

This is the historic Presbyterian answer to man's "vain imaginations," the modern cults—and the vexing problems of the human soul.

God has an answer to every need. And that answer is the Word of God illuminated by none other than the Spirit of God Himself.

9

One Church: Catholic and Reformed

THE GENTLE BREEZES of reconciliation seemed to be blowing away the seeds of bitterness which had taken root with the sixteenth-century Reformation.

Martin Bucer and Philip Melanchthon had displayed a willingness to make concessions beyond their own personal convictions as Protestants, if that would mean an end to the unrelieved hatred and bloodshed.

The Roman Catholic delegates had agreed to the idea of a married priesthood. They had also conceded that laymen henceforth receive both the bread and wine at Holy Communion.

Both sides had even reached an understanding regarding the crucial doctrine of justification by faith.

But then the much hailed Council of Ratisbon (1541) foundered on the rocky shoals of the Roman Catholic dogma of the Mass.

Bucer and Melanchthon once more sought a compromise. But the conference had been shipwrecked.

Attending the sessions only as an adviser, John Calvin wrote to his old friend Farel and told him what he thought about the entire proceedings. He made it clear that he utterly opposed the "ambiguous and insincere formulas" his Protestant colleagues had drawn up to make peace with their Roman Catholic counterparts. "So far as I can understand," wrote Calvin, "if we could be content with only a half Christ, we might easily come to understand one another."

But a half Christ. John Calvin would have none of it.

The Master of Geneva had made it indelibly clear that he would "cross ten seas," if that would help to bring about the reunion of Christ's church. "Would that the union between all Christ's churches upon Earth were such," he prayed, "that the angels in Heaven might join their song of praise."

One contemporary historian has pointed out that the word Presbyterian does not occur in a single instance in the Reformed creeds. "Calvin and the Westminster divines never said that the Presbyterian Church was *the* church," he has noted. "But they did insist that the Presbyterian Church was part of *the* church."

This astute observation is supported by the *Scots Confession,* which agrees that the "Kirk is catholic, that is, universal, because it contains the *chosen* of all ages, of all realms, nations, and tongues, be they of the Jews or be they of the Gentiles, who have communion and society with God the Father, and with His Son, Christ Jesus, through the sanctification of His Holy Spirit."

At the same time, the *Scots Confession* observed that *particular* churches, such as those at Corinth, Galatia and Ephesus, were also called the Kirks of God. "Such Kirks," it declared, "we the inhabitants of the realm of Scotland confessing Christ Jesus, do claim to have in our cities, towns, and reformed districts because of the doctrine taught in our Kirks, contained in the written Word of God . . ."

For Calvin and the other reformers, the church was to be found wherever the sacraments were rightly administered and the Word faithfully preached.

So ecumenical was the spirit of Calvin that he readily conceded that the *elect* are found within the Roman Catholic Church and that, despite corruptions, this church has preserved remnants of authentic Christianity.

"His quarrel with Rome was not the moral laxity of the Vatican or the priesthood or the monasteries, not even such abuses as the withholding of the cup from the laity or private masses," says Parker. "It was that Rome had destroyed the glory of Christ in many ways—by calling upon the saints to intercede, when Jesus Christ is the one mediator between God and man; by adoring the Blessed Virgin, when Christ alone shall be adored; by offering a continual sacrifice in the Mass, when the sacrifice of Christ upon the Cross is complete and sufficient."

Calvin put the entire matter bluntly in the *Institutes*. "It was necessary for us to withdraw from them," he says, "in order to approach Christ."

This same note is sounded in a tract Calvin addressed to Charles V. "Let our opponents, then," he says, "first of all draw near to Christ and afterwards let them accuse us of schism in daring to dissent from them in doctrine . . . We cleave to Christ rather than to them."

But the entire notion of schism in the Church of God actually repelled the spirit of this towering theologian, who likened the fellowship of believers to the *mother* of God's elect.

Calvin went so far as to insist that, if Christians claim God as their common Father and Christ as their Head, then they must also recognize the church as their *mother*.

"How useful and even necessary it is for us to know her," he says, "since there is no other way of entrance in-

111

to life, unless we are conceived by her, born of her, nourished at her breast, and continually preserved under her care and government . . ."

The great reformer further declared that God has been pleased to gather His children into the "bosom (of the church) . . . not only that they may be nourished by her help and ministry as long as they are infants and children, but also that they may be guided by her motherly care until they mature and at last reach the goal of faith. 'For what God has joined together, it is not lawful to put asunder' (Mark 10: 9), so that, for those to whom He is Father, the Church may also be Mother."

This may all sound so very "catholic" to Protestant ears. But, says Calvin, we must recognize that the church represents the unity of the Body of Christ into which we have all been engrafted. He writes:

> . . . Unless we are united with all the other members under Christ our Head, no hope of the future inheritance awaits us. Hence the Church is called catholic or universal, for two or three cannot be invented without dividing Christ; and this is impossible. All the elect of God are so joined together in Christ, that as they depend on one Head, so they are as it were compacted into one body, being knit together like its different members, made truly one by living together under the same Spirit of God in one faith, hope, and charity, called not only to the same inheritance of eternal life, but to participation in one God and Christ.

Calvin was forced to hammer out his doctrine of the church against the background of two competing heresies. Both of them sound strangely modern.

On the one hand, there was the proud and powerful Roman Catholic Church of his age, which he accused of claiming to possess the Spirit of God even as it rejected the Word of God. On the other hand, there were the Anabaptists who, he charged, had abandoned the church entirely and had become involved in "pestilent errors and pernicious reveries."

"We are assailed by two sects, which seem to differ most widely from each other," Calvin wrote in his famous letter to Cardinal James Sadolet. "For what similitude is there in appearance between the pope and the Anabaptists?

"And yet," he observes, "that you may see that Satan never transforms himself so cunningly, as not in some measure to betray himself, the principal weapon with which they both assail us, is the same.

"For when they boast extravagantly of the Spirit," he says, "the tendency certainly is to sink and bury the Word of God, that they may make room for their own falsehoods."

Calvin's charge against the Roman communion was simply this: "It is no less unreasonable to boast of the Spirit without the Word, than it would be absurd to bring forward the Word itself without the Spirit."

The true definition of the church, Calvin informed Sadolet, is that "it is the society of all the saints, a society which spread over the whole world, and existing in all ages, yet bound together by the one doctrine, and the one Spirit of Christ, cultivates and observes unity of faith and brotherly concord.

"With this church we deny that we have any disagreement," Calvin declared. "Nay, rather, as we revere our mother, so we desire to remain in her bosom."

> Elect from every nation,
>   Yet one o'er all the earth,
> Her charter of salvation,
>   One Lord, one faith, one birth.
>
> One holy Name she blesses,
>   Partakes one holy food,
> And to one hope she presses,
>   With every grace endued.

That was John Calvin's definition of the Christian church.

But that was not the concept of the church which Calvin found among the sectarian Anabaptists. "Many are urged by pride, or disdain, or envy, to persuade themselves that they can profit sufficiently by reading and meditating in private, and so to despise public assemblies, and consider preaching as unnecessary," he observed.

"But since they do all in their power to dissolve and break asunder the bond of unity," he warned, ". . . not one of them escapes the just punishment of this impious breach . . ."

John Calvin's words ring as clear today as they did in the sixteenth century. For he was both *ecumenical* and *evangelical*. He preached one church—Catholic and Reformed.

The Master of Geneva would have some pretty strong words for those who think that they can skip worship services because they get more spiritual benefit from sitting in front of the tv on Sunday morning. Calvin would be the first to shout loud and clear that there is no such animal as the solitary Christian. Alcoholics Anonymous there might be, but Christians Anonymous, no!

Nor would he accept the notion that every man has a right to his own beliefs where the Gospel is concerned. To correct such error, Calvin would have probably quoted II Peter 1: 20, 21: "Knowing this first, that no prophecy of the scripture is of any private interpretation. For the prophecy came not in old time by the will of man: but holy men of God spake as they were moved by the Holy Ghost."

"Here, therefore," says Calvin, "it is necessary to remember that, whatever authority and dignity is attributed by the Holy Spirit . . . it is given, not in a strict sense to the persons themselves, but to the *ministry* over which they were appointed, or, to speak more correctly, to the

114

Word, the ministration of which was committed to them."

Calvin understood the ministry of the Word to be committed to pastors and teachers, who, he said, "are always indispensable to the church." For they are charged with the responsibility of "the interpretation of the Scripture, that pure and sound doctrine may be retained among believers." Says Calvin:

> This is the extent of the power with which the pastors of the church . . . ought to be invested—that by the Word of God they may . . . build up the house of Christ, and subvert the house of Satan; may feed the sheep, and drive away the wolves; may instruct and exhort the docile; may reprove, rebuke, and restrain the rebellious and obstinate; may bind and loose; may discharge their lightnings and thunders, if necessary, but all in the Word of God.

It soon becomes clear that John Calvin believed in a strong and capable educated ministry. He knew only too well that, if Scripture could be proclaimed by "private interpretation, a tyranny worse than that of Rome would soon infect the whole church.

Therefore, he pleaded for a strong church government, administered equally by duly ordained ministers and laymen. "If no society, and even no house, though containing only a small family, can be preserved in a proper state without discipline," he says, "this is far more necessary in the church, the state of which ought to be the most orderly of all.

"As the saving doctrine of Christ is the soul of the church," he writes, "so discipline forms the ligaments which connect the members together, and keep each in its proper place."

The notion of freewheeling churchmanship ran completely counter to Calvin's understanding of Scripture. "Discipline . . . serves as a bridle to curb . . . (those) who resist the doctrine of Christ," he says, "or as a spur to stimulate the inactive; and sometimes as a father's rod, with which those who have grievously fallen may be chastised in mercy, and with the gentleness of the Spirit of Christ."

Calvin followed the apostle in setting down the methods and course of disciplinary action. The initial approach to the offender should be through private admonitions, he says. But if the offender persists, then Calvin recommends excommunication—a word all but obsolete in most Protestant churches today.

"But it ought not to be forgotten," says Calvin, "that the severity becoming the church must be tempered with a spirit of gentleness . . . To comprehend all in a word, let us not condemn to eternal death the person himself, who is in the hand and power of God alone, but let us content ourselves with judging of the nature of his works according to the law of the Lord . . ."

How many churches today would avoid disunity and trouble if only they followed Calvin as Calvin followed the Bible on these points. For the goal of church discipline, says Paul, is "speaking the truth in love, [we all] may grow up into him in all things, which is the head, even Christ" (Ephesians 4: 15).

While Calvin was writing primarily for those of the Reformed churches, there is no doubt that he was thinking of the Anabaptists and the Roman communion as well.

One of his principle charges against the Anabaptists was that they promoted independence run amok. They had, in his opinion, allowed their liberty in Christ to degenerate into a kind of dangerous license. One group, for example, had resorted to the practice of polygamy.

His stand against the Roman Catholic Church is, in some ways, more conciliatory. He deeply disliked the very thought of schism. But perversions of the Gospel within that church forced him to follow Luther in the way of reform. One can only guess what Calvin would think of so many Protestant churches in our own age, which have retained the husk of the Gospel but thrown the seed away.

When it came to relationships with other Reformed churches, John Calvin represented the epitome of a truly evangelical ecumenical churchman. He and Luther traded books and, while they never met one another, mutual friends would pass on the word, "Salute Doctor Martin respectfully in my name." Calvin referred to the older Luther as "my much respected father."

This may explain why Presbyterians have always been in the vanguard along the rocky road to Christian unity.

"I was once permitted to unite in celebrating the Lord's Supper in an upper room in Jerusalem," the great Scottish minister Robert Murray McCheyne once wrote. "There were fourteen present, the most of whom, I had good reason to believe, knew and loved the Lord Jesus Christ. Several were godly Episcopalians, two were converted Jews, and one a Christian from Nazareth, converted under the American missionaries.

"The bread and wine were dispensed in the Episcopal manner, and most were kneeling as they received them," says McCheyne. "Perhaps . . . (you) would have shrunk back with horror, and called this the confusion of Babel.

"We felt it to be sweet fellowship with Christ and with the brethren," he writes. "And as we left the upper room, and looked out upon the Mount of Olives, we remembered with calm joy the prayer of our Lord that ascended from one of its shady ravines, after the first Lord's Supper: 'Neither pray I for these alone, but for them also which shall believe in Me through their word, that they all may be ONE.' "

This interest in Christian unity has continued among Presbyterians down to the present day. But its only basis can be, as McCheyne observed, in and through "sweet fellowship with Christ and with the brethren." Any other basis is sure to fail.

117

Unfortunately, this very desire to be faithful to Christ and to one's own convictions has sometimes led to division within the Presbyterian household itself. On other occasions, division can be attributed to social and cultural factors.

At any rate, there are still about a dozen Presbyterian bodies in the United States alone. This figure does not include those churches which bear the title of Reformed. However, efforts are constantly underway to bring about unity in this household of faith.

The major Presbyterian body is the United Presbyterian Church in the U.S.A., a merger of the Presbyterian Church in the U.S.A. and the United Presbyterian Church of North America. The first body traces its lineage back to the days of Makemie and Witherspoon, while the second took pride in its direct descent from the Covenantors of Scotland. The merger took place in 1958. Today the United Presbyterians number about three million.

The Presbyterian Church in the United States is known colloquially as the Southern Presbyterian Church. It was founded at the time of the War Between the States. Ongoing efforts have been made to bring about a merger of this largely conservative body with the more liberal United Presbyterians. The Southern Presbyterians have about 900,000 members.

Presbyterian interest in Christian unity has been matched by an interest in Christian missions.

The names of David Brainerd, Marcus Whitman and Sheldon Jackson stand out as missionaries to the American Indian and settlers beyond the Rockies.

But the Presbyterians of the United States and Europe also recognized that there was a world to bring to Christ. Alexander Duff was therefore sent to India by the Church of Scotland, J. W. Heron and Horace G. Underwood to Korea by the American Presbyterians, Samuel M. Zwemer to the Near East by the Reformed Church in America, and David Livingstone to Africa after receiving the call in Scotland.

Today Presbyterian missionaries—or fraternal workers —are to be found in the far-off corners of the world, building upon the foundation left by these early pioneers.

However, the name of David Livingstone still ranks among the most widely known and best loved Christian statesmen of the modern missionary movement. So it was that President Kenneth D. Kaunda of Zambia unveiled a plaque in May, 1973, to commemorate the centennial of Livingstone's death and to demonstrate that his countrymen had not forgotten the man who opened up the Dark Continent, fought the slave trade, and at last died on his knees in prayer in the vast land he loved so well.

What was the secret power of this great geographer and medical missionary?

"For a long time I felt much depressed after preaching the unsearchable riches of Christ to apparently insensible hearts," he declared. "But now I like to dwell on the love of the great Mediator. For it always warms my heart, and I know that the Gospel is the power of God—the great means which He employs for the regeneration of our ruined world."

Presbyterians also know that this love—this power of the Gospel—is also the way to unity and to the visible demonstration of One Church: Catholic and Reformed.

10

Accepted in the Beloved!

GEORGE GALLUP might not be too far off the mark when he suggests that human reason could "prove God statistically."

But that is small comfort to the person—adult or teenager—who needs and yearns for a God great enough to meet his deepest longings and most trying tribulations. After all, it isn't easy to place one's very life in the care of a philosophical abstraction or to have much confidence in a mere statistic.

Moreover, John Calvin would turn over in his grave if he learned that someone was trying to do God a service by actually *reducing* Him to the relatively manageable limits of statistical probability.

It is true, as Calvin would readily admit, that "the invisible things of him from the creation of the world are clearly seen, being understood by the things that are made, even his eternal power and Godhead" (Romans 1: 20).

But this *natural knowledge* is a far step from any *saving knowledge* of God. It simply leaves man, as the apostle declares, "without excuse" for willful unbelief. "We cannot with propriety say," says Calvin, "there is any knowledge of God where there is no religion or piety."

However, "religion or piety" comes hard to a man whose god is a statistic or abstraction. Love and devotion are reserved alone for persons—persons whom we encounter and with whom we can enter into fellowship and joyful communion.

The glory of Israel rested in the glory of her God. He is not the far-off deity of the heathen. He is rather "a friend that sticketh closer than a brother" (Proverbs 18:24). So intimate was the relationship between God and His ancient people that it could be written:

> Our help is in the Name of the Lord, who made Heaven and Earth.
> The eternal God is thy Refuge, and underneath are the everlasting arms.
> Like as a father pitieth his children, so the Lord pitieth them that fear Him.
> As one whom his mother comforteth, so will I comfort you; and ye shall be comforted.
> God is our Refuge and Strength, a very present Help in trouble. Therefore will not we fear.

This knowledge of a God who cares and understands still brings comfort and hope to those who stand before the open grave of a loved one, whenever a United Presbyterian minister reads these Old Testament texts from *The Book of Common Worship* during the funeral service.

But the Christian experience has been that God, "who at sundry times and in divers manners spake in time past unto the fathers by the prophets, Hath in these last days spoken unto us by His Son." Of this Son, the writer of Hebrews declares:

> (God) hath appointed (Him) heir of all things, by

whom also he made the worlds; Who being the brightness of his glory, and the express image of his person, and upholding all things by the word of his power, when he had by himself purged our sins, sat down on the right hand of the Majesty on high (Hebrews 1: 1-3).

The miracle of Christmas is that God was not content to remain aloof from sinful, sorrowing man as "a most pure spirit, invisible, without body, parts or passions." The Creator rather sought to identify personally with His lost creation at the deepest levels of human need. So it was that "God sent . . . his Son into the world . . . that the world through him might be saved" (John 3: 17).

And the Word was *made flesh,* and dwelt among us, (and we beheld his glory, the glory as of the only begotten of the Father,) full of grace and truth (John 1: 14).

The Good News that God became flesh—literally "one of us"—is known to the theologians as the miracle of the Incarnation. Matthew records this great event in these words:

And [Mary] shall bring forth a son, and thou shalt call his name JESUS: for he shall save his people from their sins. Now all this was done, that it might be fulfilled which was spoken of the Lord by the prophet, saying, Behold, a virgin shall be with child, and shall bring forth a son, and they shall call his name *Emmanuel,* which being interpreted is, God with us (Matthew 1: 21-23).

Such stupendous news was not readily understood or accepted in the ancient world, anymore than it is readily understood or accepted by people today. But, said Paul, this Gospel of Christ "is the power of God unto salvation to every one that believeth; to the Jew first, and also to the Greek" (Romans 1: 16).

The problem was that the Jew, unlike his pagan neighbors, found all that he thought he needed to know about

God in his ancient confession, the *Shema*: *Shema Yisroel Adonoi Elohenu Adonai Echod*—Hear, O Israel, the Lord our God, The Lord Is One. If this was true, then it was difficult for the Jew to believe that God had a Son. And it was downright blasphemy from the Jewish perspective for Jesus Himself to declare: "I and my Father are one" (John 10: 30).

Those in the Gentile world faced a problem of a different sort. Having been raised in a pagan culture that included many objects of worship, Gentile converts sometimes had the tendency to place Jesus alongside the other gods with which they were familiar. But Christ demanded more than that. And His apostles insisted that Jesus was due the same honor and respect among Christians that Jehovah received within the Household of Israel. More cultured Gentiles simply dismissed the Gospel as a pious flight of fancy. Therefore, St. Paul wrote:

> For the preaching of the cross is to them that perish foolishness . . . For the Jews require a sign, and the Greeks seek after wisdom: But we preach Christ crucified, unto the Jews a stumblingblock, and unto the Greeks foolishness; But unto them which are called, both Jews and Greeks, Christ the power of God, and the wisdom of God (I Corinthians 1: 18, 22-24).

Some have claimed that the beauty of this Good News somehow gets lost in the so-called rigid theology of John Calvin. He seems to be forever concerned with the absolute sovereignty of God, they argue, and those *eternal decrees* to elect some to salvation and others to damnation.

But nothing could be further from the truth. "The centrality of Christ is . . . the first fact to be noticed in Calvin's theology," says Parker. "(It is found) in its scientific form in the *Institutes* and in its pastoral form in the Sermons."

"There is nothing that Satan so much tries to effect as to call up mists so as to obscure Christ," says Calvin himself. ". . . He knows that by this means the way is opened up for every kind of falsehood.

"This, therefore," he writes, "is the only means of retaining, as well as restoring, pure doctrine: to place Christ before the view such as He is with all His blessings, that His excellence may be truly perceived."

Calvin embarks upon this theological goal by first pointing out that it is impossible to know God as our Father because "our conscience disturbs us within, and convinces us that our sins afford a just reason why God should abandon us, and no longer esteem us as His children."

This is not some kind of theological double-talk. It is rather a fact which we all have experienced in the midst of our sin and failures. When we can no longer accept ourselves, we find it impossible to believe that God can accept us either.

But the Good News of the Gospel is that *God does accept us* in spite of ourselves. In fact, says St. Paul, God has "predestinated us unto the adoption of children by Jesus Christ to himself, according to the good pleasure of his will, To the praise of the glory of his grace, wherein he hath made us accepted in the beloved. In whom we have redemption through his blood, the forgiveness of sins, according to the riches of his grace" (Ephesians 1: 5-7).

The New Testament uses a series of contrasts to demonstrate the radical transformation that occurs in the life of the person who has experienced this act of redemption—this new birth—offered by God to us in Jesus Christ:

You were dead . . . but now are alive.
You were guilty . . . but now are forgiven.
You were a sinner . . . but now are made righteous.

You were condemned . . . but now are pardoned.
You were lost . . . but now are found.
You were alienated . . . but now are reconciled.
You were a slave . . . but now are free.
You once were a stranger . . . but now are an heir.

But, like the kids say, there's Only One Way! "There can be no *saving knowledge* of God without Christ," says Calvin. "And, consequently . . . from the beginning of the world, He has always been manifested to the elect, that they might look to Him, and repose all their confidence in Him."

It is possible that John Calvin was thinking of Abraham offering his son Isaac upon the altar of sacrifice. But so great an offering was unnecessary for a God who Himself provided the lamb. Therefore, Jesus informed the Jews of His day: "Your father Abraham rejoiced to see my day: and he saw it, and was glad.

"Verily, verily," declared our Lord, ". . . Before Abraham was, I am" (John 8: 56, 58).

No One other than the Son of God Himself is "the Lamb slain from the foundation of the world" (Revelation 13: 8).

However, says Calvin, "it was of great importance to our interests that He, who was to be our Mediator, should be both true God and true man.

"Our situation was truly deplorable," he writes, "unless the Divine Majesty itself would descend to us. For we could not ascend to it . . . So great was the (gulf) between our pollution and the perfect purity of God."

For Calvin, that breach could only be spanned by Immanuel, the God who became one of us in the person of His only begotten Son. Through His incarnation, he says, God took "to Himself what belongs to us, and transfer(red) to us that which is His, and (made) that which is His by nature ours by grace!"

In that act, says Calvin, the "heirs of hell" were transformed into the "heirs of the Kingdom of God."

He who was righteousness itself became sin for us. He who was life itself swallowed up death. "Now," asks Calvin, "who possesses life or righteousness . . . but God alone?"

However, Calvin recognized that it is easier for people to concede the deity of Christ than it is to accept His full humanity. "They reckon it base and dishonoring to Christ to have derived His descent from men, because, in that case, He could not be exempted from the common law which includes the whole offspring of Adam without exception under sin," he observes.

"But this difficulty is easily solved by Paul's antithesis, 'As by one man sin entered into the world, and death by sin'—'even so by the righteousness of one the free gift came upon all men unto justification of life" (Romans 5: 12, 18)."

So it is that John Calvin followed in the tradition of the framers of the great creeds of the early church, insisting upon the true deity and the true humanity of the Son of God who became the Son of man.

It becomes readily apparent that Calvin rejected the notion that Christ was just a great man among other men in the same way that he rejected the notion that He was less than a man. Either He was the God-Man, or He was nothing.

"Although heretics profess the name of Christ, yet He is not a foundation to them in common with the pious," he writes. "Christ will be found among them only in name, not in reality."

This is a common problem among so-called Christians in every age. They may claim to follow Christ as a great prophet, leader or example. But they know nothing of His resurrection power in their daily lives. Hence, they cannot testify with Paul: "I am crucified with Christ: nevertheless I live; yet not I, but Christ liveth in me: and the life which I now live in the flesh I live by the faith of the Son of God, who loved me, and gave himself for me" (Galatians 2: 20).

"Therefore," says Calvin, "that faith may find in Christ a solid ground of salvation, and so may rely on Him, it is proper for us to establish . . . that the office which was assigned to Him by the Father consists of three parts. For He was given as a Prophet, a King, and a Priest."

Fanny Crosby, the blind hymnwriter, was thinking of this threefold office of Christ when she penned the words of that beautiful tribute to her Savior and Lord:

Praise Him! Praise Him! Jesus, our blessed Redeemer!
Heavenly portals loud with hosannas ring!
Jesus, Saviour, reigneth forever and ever;
Crown Him! Crown Him! Prophet and Priest and King!

The Bible itself reveals that, while other men in times past had been chosen by God to assume these roles, the Messiah would come as the perfect prophet, the perfect priest, and the perfect king in making salvation available to a sinful and despairing world.

Charles Hodge, the distinguished American Presbyterian theologian, points out that these three offices were separate and distinct in the Old Testament. "The prophet, as such, was not a priest," he writes. "And the king was neither priest nor prophet."

However, Dr. Hodge further observes that there were occasions when one person did assume more than a single role. For example, Moses was both priest and prophet, while David served as both prophet and king.

Nevertheless, says Dr. Hodge, the ancient Jew understood that the promised Messiah would incorporate within Himself all three mediatorial functions. This great Princeton scholar comments:

Moses, speaking of Christ, said, "The Lord thy God will raise up unto thee a prophet from the midst of

127

thee, of thy brethren, like unto me." It was abundantly taught that the coming deliverer was to discharge all the duties of a prophet as a revealer of the will of God. He was to be the great teacher of righteousness; a light to lighten the Gentiles as well as the glory of His people Israel. No less clearly and frequently was it declared that He should be a priest. "Thou art a priest forever after the order of Melchizedec." He was to be a priest upon his throne (Zechariah 6: 13). He was to bear the sins of the people, and make intercession for transgressors. His royal office is rendered so prominent in the Messianic prophecies that the Jews looked for Him only as a king. He was to reign over all nations. Of his kingdom there was to be no end. He was to be the Lord of lords and the King of kings.

Christians believe that Jesus of Nazareth fulfilled these long-held expectations as the promised Messiah of God. Charles Wesley wrote a beautiful Advent hymn to summarize this deep conviction:

> Come, Thou long expected Jesus,
>   Born to set Thy people free;
> From our fears and sins release us;
>   Let us find our rest in Thee.
> Israel's Strength and Consolation,
>   Hope of all the world Thou art;
> Dear Desire of every nation,
>   Joy of every longing heart.
>
> Born Thy people to deliver,
>   Born a child and yet a King.
> Born to reign in us forever,
>   Now Thy gracious kingdom bring.
> By Thine own eternal Spirit
>   Rule in all our hearts alone;
> By Thine all-sufficient merit,
>   Raise us to Thy glorious throne.

As a prophet, says Calvin, Christ was commissioned by the Father to be a witness of His grace. He points out that the Lord Jesus ascribed to Himself the words of

Isaiah at the very outset of His ministry:

> The Spirit of the Lord is upon me, because he hath anointed me to preach the gospel to the poor; he hath sent me to heal the brokenhearted, to preach deliverance to the captives, and recovering of sight to the blind, to set at liberty them that are bruised, To preach the acceptable year of the Lord (Luke 4: 18, 19).

"The tendency of the prophetic dignity in Christ is," says Calvin, "to assure us that all the branches of perfect wisdom are included in the system of doctrine which He has given us." In a word, Jesus Christ tells us all we need to know about the Father and His gracious plan for our salvation, which He "prepared for *you* from the foundation of the world" (Matthew 25: 34).

So it is, says Calvin, that even as king, Jesus Christ "reigns for *us* rather than for Himself." But this does not mean that the Christian life on Earth will be any bed of roses.

"Whatever . . . is promised us in Christ," he remarks, "consists not in . . . a life of joy and tranquility, abundant wealth, security from every injury, and numerous delights suited to our carnal desires . . .

"Christ (rather) enriches His people with everything necessary for the eternal salvation of their souls," he explains, "and arms them with strength to enable them to stand invincible against all the assaults of their spiritual foes."

This may sound like no more than the promise of a pie-in-the-sky-in-the-sweet-by-and-by. But Christian experience testifies to the fact that our King provides this strength to meet the hard tests of the here-and-now.

"In the world ye shall have tribulation," said our Lord. "But be of good cheer; I have overcome the world" (John 16: 33). We can, therefore, rest in His promise: "Peace I leave with you, my peace I give unto you: not as the world giveth, give I unto you. Let not your heart be troubled, neither let it be afraid" (John 14: 27).

As Christians, we may watch as others attain greater power, popularity and wealth, while we ourselves carry burdens which sometimes seem too heavy to bear. But so did our Lord. His Cross came before the crown. And so it may be with us.

However, asks James, "Hath not God chosen the poor of this world rich in faith, and heirs of the kingdom which he hath promised to them that love him?" (James 2: 5). Therefore, our faith is simply this:

Pardon for sin and a peace that endureth,
    Thine own dear presence to cheer and to guide;
Strength for today and bright hope for tomorrow,
    Blessings all mine, with ten thousand beside!

At the same time, it becomes clear for Calvin that this present peace and the hope for the glorious destiny as "heirs of the kingdom" could not be offered by one who was merely a great example or an influence for good in a ruined world.

Sinful man is separated from his all-holy Maker. Therefore, says Calvin, we need a mediator—a priest— who by his own holiness "may render us acceptable to God."

"In order that our Priest may appease the wrath of God, and procure His favor for us, there is a necessity for the intervention of an atonement," he writes. "Wherefore, that Christ might perform this office, it was necessary for Him to appear with a sacrifice."

Someone has said that God hates sin but loves the sinner. Therefore, says Paul, our great High Priest, "who knew no sin; [became sin for us] that we might be made the righteousness of God in him" (II Corinthians 5: 21).

That is the basis of God's plan for our salvation. God Himself took the sinner's place in the atonement that we

130

might be made one with Him. "The love of God the Father therefore precedes our reconciliation in Christ," says Calvin. "Or rather it is because He first loves that He afterwards reconciles us to Himself."

"He surrendered Himself to death to be subdued," he declares, "not that He might be overwhelmed by its power, but rather that He might overthrow that which threatened us."

But it would be small comfort to the Christian if death ended the whole story. Thankfully, it does not!

"Our salvation is perfectly accomplished by His death," explains Calvin, "yet we are said to have been 'begotten again to a lively hope,' not by His death, but 'by His resurrection from the dead.'

"It is on His resurrection that our faith principally rests," he writes. ". . . Wherefore we ascribe our salvation partly to the death of Christ, and partly to His resurrection.

"We believe that sin was abolished, and death destroyed, by the former," he says, "(and) that righteousness was restored, and life established, by the latter."

Those who have put their faith and trust in Christ—and in Him alone—can therefore exult with Paul: "For to me to live is Christ, and to die is gain" (Philippians 1: 21). But of those who reject God's gracious offer in His Son, the writer of Hebrews asks: "How shall we escape, if we neglect so great salvation?" (Hebrews 2: 3).

"We as fallen men, ignorant, guilty, polluted, and helpless, need a Savior who is a prophet to instruct us; a priest to atone and to make intercession for us; and a king to rule over and protect us," declares Charles Hodge. ". . . . Our Redeemer is to us at once (that) prophet, priest, and king."

It is this sturdy faith which assures us that we have indeed been "accepted in the Beloved!"

11

The Gospel in the Tulip

No one paid very much attention to the little girl as the giant ocean liner heaved under the heavy swells that almost lifted the vessel out of the water, then battered it with fury.

Some of the older passengers turned white as they awaited the worst. Even some of the seasoned crew members prepared for a possible disaster on the high seas.

But then a middle-aged woman noticed the child curled up in a deck chair, seemingly oblivious to the impending peril. "You're a brave little girl," the woman managed to remark in the midst of her own panic. "Why aren't you afraid?"

"Why should I be afraid?" the youngster replied. "My father is the captain."

That's what Presbyterian theology is all about.

But that's not the impression one would get by discussing the teachings of John Calvin with the average person on Main Street, U.S.A.

If the name of the great Reformer elicited anything other than a blank stare, the chances are that one of two things would occur. Either Calvin's ghost would conjure up a vision of a peaches-and-cream Doris Day singing *Que Sera, Sera,* "Whatever will be will be . . ." Or there would be the nightmare of Salem witches roasting unbaptized babies in hell.

In academic circles, Calvin and his successors would be charged with promoting a kind of blind fatalism or "theological determinism."

Just what do they mean by theological determinism?

In Calvin's case, they mean that the great Reformer taught that God *determined* from eternity to eternity just who will be heirs of hell and who will inherit the Kingdom of Heaven. Man, it is insisted, can't do very much about the matter. For his eternal destiny has already been sealed in the counsels of the Almighty.

It must be admitted that Calvin himself indeed defined *predestination* as "the eternal decree of God, by which He has determined in Himself what He would have to become of every individual of mankind."

"For they are not all created with a similar destiny," he declared. "But eternal life is fore-ordained for some, and eternal damnation for others."

Calvin would not even concede that *election* is based upon the fact that God knows beforehand just who will accept His unmerited grace and who will reject His plan of salvation. Rather, says Calvin, God *determines* in the counsels of His own will who will be saved and who will be lost.

In fairness to Calvin, however, it must be pointed out that St. Augustine long centuries before had given this doctrine its distinctive shape, while Thomas Aquinas taught it just as boldly and clearly as the Master of Geneva.

Moreover, it is extremely significant that Calvin doesn't even discuss these *eternal decrees* until he has first considered the person and work of Jesus Christ and life in the Spirit. He only considers this "great mystery" after first outlining his doctrines of justification by faith and the work of the Holy Spirit in the believer's heart.

At the same time, Calvin warned that the doctrine of predestination itself was "rather intricate" and "therefore dangerous." He feared that many would allow "human curiosity" to run wild and wander "into forbidden labyrinths . . . as if determined to leave none of the Divine secrets unscrutinized and unexplored . . ."

Unfortunately, many of Calvin's followers failed to heed their mentor's warning. They proceeded to out-Calvin Calvin, some even going so far as to suggest that God *elected* some to *damnation* even before He *elected* to provide *salvation* by grace in Christ Jesus.

That is what the Synod of Dort was all about.

Jacob Arminius had strongly protested against the hyper-Calvinism of some of his fellow faculty members at the University of Leyden. The ensuing feud centered around what became known as the Five Points of Calvinism. They're really easy to remember:

> Total depravity.
> Unconditional election.
> Limited atonement.
> Irresistible grace.
> Perseverance of the saints.

Put them all together and you have John Calvin's "Gospel in the T-U-L-I-P."

However, Arminius completely rejected the notions of *unconditional election* and *irresistible grace*. He rather insisted that these two doctrines deny man's freedom of choice to either accept or reject God's gracious offer of salvation in Jesus Christ.

Therefore, Arminius and his supporters issued a series

of *Remonstrants,* which have since become known as the Five Points of Arminianism. These *Remonstrants* declared:

1. Election and condemnation are conditioned upon the faith or unbelief of every individual.
2. Salvation through Christ is *for all men,* but only believers enjoy its benefits.
3. Man is unable to come to God unless he is aided by the Holy Spirit.
4. The grace of God is not irresistible.
5. It is open to question whether those who have once experienced salvation can ultimately be lost.

In the end, Arminianism was condemned in the Netherlands. However, there are many who still accept the teachings of this once-banished Dutch theologian. Among them are the Methodists and members of other Wesleyan bodies.

However, Calvin himself, no less than his sometimes overly enthusiastic followers, saw clearly that far more was at stake than the mere freedom of sinful man. He rather recognized that the absolute sovereignty of God, the very keystone of his understanding of theology, was involved in this "great mystery."

What Calvin sought to demonstrate from the Bible was that salvation comes through God's initiative and His alone. "For by grace are ye saved through faith; and that not of yourselves: it is the gift of God: Not of works, lest any man should boast" (Ephesians 2: 8, 9).

Man is no less dependent upon God for the gift of faith than he is for the gift of grace. In fact, both are but two sides of the same coin.

Therefore, Wilhelm Pauck, a noted contemporary theologian, has pointed out that *predestination* must be understood in light of the salvation we have *experienced* in Christ, and not on the basis of man's speculation about the nature of God.

"If man is redeemed only by the initiative of a gracious, merciful God, it must also be said that his eternal destiny is *determined* by God," says Pauck. "The doctrine of *predestination* therefore stands in an immediate context with that of grace and with that of original sin.

"It is designed," he explains, "in order to give doctrinal expression to the religious conviction that man is altogether dependent upon God for his salvation."

Thus Calvinism knows nothing of man's climb upward and onward to God. Its followers only know of the absolute Sovereign of the universe coming down to man in the person of His Son—Immanuel, God with us.

At the same time, Calvin and his disciples believed that this "insider's secret" about the grace of God could be proved by what they saw about them in daily life. For, while there were those who readily accepted the Gospel, others seemed to be incapable of responding to the Good News in Jesus Christ.

The very fact that a person has a deep concern about his soul's salvation is pretty good evidence that the Holy Spirit is convicting him of sin and calling him to salvation and a life of righteousness in Christ.

Moreover, the young person or adult who simply trusts God as his Father, and accepts Christ as his Savior and Lord, never has to worry one bit about whether he is one of God's elect. His very faith provides the assurance. Paul puts the entire matter like this:

For as many as are led by the Spirit of God, they are the sons of God . . . And we know that all things work together for good to them that love God, to them who are the called according to his purpose. For whom he did foreknow, he also did predestinate to be conformed to the image of his Son, that he might be the firstborn among many brethren. Moreover whom he did predestinate, them he also called: and whom he called, them he also justified: and whom he justified, them he also glorified.

What shall we then say to these things? If God be for us, who can be against us? He that spared not his own Son, but delivered him up for us all, how shall he not with him also freely give us all things? Who shall lay any thing to the charge of God's elect? It is God that justifieth. Who is he that condemneth? (Romans 8: 14, 28-34).

This does not mean that the most stalwart saint won't have his moments of doubt and even experience that "dark night of the soul." But the testimony of Scripture is that we are not saved by our *feelings,* but rather by the *fact* of our blessed Lord's sacrificial death and glorious resurrection.

"For I am persuaded," says Paul, "that neither death, nor life, nor angels, nor principalities, nor powers, nor things present, nor things to come, Nor height, nor depth, nor any other creature, shall be able to separate us from the love of God, which is in Christ Jesus our Lord" (Romans 8: 38, 39).

With that assurance, let's take an "insider's" view of the Gospel in the Tulip.

T stands for total depravity. This does not mean that man doesn't have some good intentions. Nor does it imply that every thought and action is wholly evil. But it does mean that man's best efforts and motives are made impure by sin and self-interest.

If this sounds terribly pessimistic, we have only to remember the psalmist's lament: "Behold, I was shapen in iniquity; and in sin did my mother conceive me" (Psalm 51: 5). We further find the prophet making the firm declaration that "all our righteousnesses are as filthy rags" (Isaiah 64: 6). To which the apostle adds: "There is none that doeth good, no, not one" (Romans 3: 12).

Man is both Doctor Jekyll and Mister Hyde. He may be capable of some good; but he is also capable of committing the grossest crimes. Nero fiddled while Rome burned. And modern monsters listened to Beethoven as thousands upon thousands of innocents were led to the gas chambers.

It actually took two world wars to convince some people that man is not as good as they had insisted. As a result, they were forced to concede that the Bible displays a remarkable realism regarding the so-called human condition.

Something more than "goodwill" and "social betterment" is needed to lift man out of spiritual darkness.

Sweden, for example, is one of the four richest countries in the world. It has no slums. It boasts the finest educational and social security programs. But, said a recent issue of *Eternity* magazine, "Happiness isn't Sweden."

According to an official government report, 25 percent of the Swedish population is in need of psychiatric services. Alcoholism has risen 424 percent in the past decade. Suicide has practically doubled during that same period.

Yet, observed *Eternity,* "if wealth, security and education could guarantee happiness and contentment, Sweden would be a virtual paradise."

Is it just possible that the Bible has the answer for men who are spiritually dead? Our Lord said simply: "Ye must be born again" (John 3: 7).

U stands for unconditional election. The difference between the church and the world is that the church believes that men can be redeemed. The world isn't quite so sure. To prove this point, all one has to do is to consider just how the world treats the ex-convict, the alcoholic, the kid hooked on drugs, or the girl with an out-of-wedlock pregnancy.

Against such cynicism, the Christian displays an optimism rooted not in man but in God. "To despair of man is not unchristian—far from it," says J. S. Whale. "But to despair of man in such a way that you are really despairing of God is blasphemy. Indeed, it is atheism!"

Therefore, the Calvinist turns to his Bible and rejoices in the knowledge of unconditional election. God doesn't choose us on the basis of our wealth, our power, or our prestige. He doesn't even choose us on the basis of our own presumed goodness. Rather, He saves us "freely by his grace through the redemption that is in Christ Jesus" (Romans 3: 24).

When we get to Heaven, we're just as likely to find Mary O'Grady as the Colonel's Lady. The cop *or* the robber. The pauper rather than the prince. Robert Murray McCheyne testified to God's unconditional election in these words:

> Chosen not for good in me,
>   Wakened up from wrath to flee,
> Hidden in the Saviour's side,
>   By the Spirit sanctified,
> Teach me, Lord, on earth to show,
>   By my love, how much I owe.

L stands for limited atonement. While the Bible declares that "whosoever will may come," the Calvinist understands that the invitation is *made* to all, but only *efficacious* for some.

Here we are faced with a paradox. Critics of Calvinism claim that the doctrine of predestination destroys the notion of human freedom. But the Calvinist knows that God could have so created man so that all men would have submitted to His sovereignty. However, this He would not do because that would have been to deny man the freedom to either accept or reject Him. God does not want robots. He wants real people to love Him on the basis of His own unconditional love!

> My soul is dark, my heart is steel,
>   I cannot hear, I cannot feel,
> For light, for life, I must appeal,
>   In simple faith to Jesus.

139

Some will be touched by the convicting power of the Holy Spirit calling them to repentance and faith. Others will not. So it was that the joy of the new birth burst upon the souls of the woman taken in adultery, the despised Zacchaeus, and the unlettered disciples. But Herod, Pilate, and Judas remained in spiritual darkness—even though they had been personally confronted by the Master.

Try as we may, we cannot erase such Biblical references as those concerning "His sheep" (John 10: 11, 15), "His Church" (Acts 20: 28; Ephesians 5: 25-27), "His people" (Matthew 1: 21), and "the elect" (Romans 8: 32-35).

Our Lord Himself very definitely limited the scope of His atoning death, when He said, "I pray not for the world, but for them which thou hast given me" (John 17: 9). "Why should He limit His intercessory prayer," asks the Calvinist, "if He had actually paid the price for all?"

Charles Hodge, the great Princeton theologian, readily admits that the atonement is *sufficient* for all. But it is *efficient* only for some. He offers these illustrations:

> If a ship containing the wife and children of a man standing on the shore is wrecked, he may seize a boat and hasten to their rescue. His motive is love to his family; his purpose is to save them. But the boat which he has provided may be large enough to receive the whole of the ship's company. Would there be any inconsistency in his offering them the opportunity to escape? And if any or all of those to whom the offer was made, should refuse to accept it . . . —some because they did not duly appreciate their danger, (and) some because they thought they could save themselves—their guilt and folly would be just as great as though the man had no regard to his own family, and no special purpose to effect their deliverance.
>
> Or, a man may make a feast for his own friends, and the provision be so abundant that he may throw

140

open his doors to all who are willing to come. This is precisely what God . . . has actually done. Out of special love to His people, and with the design of securing their salvation, He has sent His Son to do what justifies the offer of salvation to all who choose to accept it. Christ, therefore, did not die equally for all men. *He laid down His life for His sheep. He gave Himself for His Church.* But in perfect consistency with all this, He did all that was necessary . . ., all that is required for the salvation of all men. So that all (Calvinists) can join with the Synod of Dort in saying, *'No man perishes for want of an atonement.'*

I stands for irresistible grace. God pursues those whom He calls as the Hound of Heaven. They may have rejected Him and rebelled against His sovereign will. But ultimately they will be drawn to a knowledge of His Son by the cords of Divine love.

John Newton was a slave trader. God called, and Newton came.

Nicky Cruz was a gang leader. God called, and Nicky came.

And there are countless thousands the world over— good and bad, rich and poor, educated and illiterate, young and old, men and women—and they'll all tell you one thing: The grace of God is irresistible. John Newton put it like this:

> Amazing grace! how sweet the sound,
>   That saved a wretch like me!
> I once was lost, but now am found,
>   Was blind, but now I see.
>
> 'Twas grace that taught my heart to fear,
>   And grace my fears relieved;
> How precious did that grace appear
>   The hour I first believed!

Have you ever watched a construction crew tear a huge gaping hole in the ground? You find it impossible to visualize the new building that will someday stand on that barren and battered piece of real estate. But if you look yonder, you will see the architect with the blueprints. He looks beyond the concrete and steel and sees a towering monument to his own genius. And so it is with the sovereign election and irresistible grace of God! Egbert Watson Smith has aptly observed:

> . . . Before creation's dawn, before the morning stars sang together or the sons of God shouted for joy, away back "in the beginning," God had a thought of me, and that thought was love. Before He found a place for the universe in His hand, He had found a place for me in His heart. As He says in Jeremiah, "Yea, I have loved thee with an everlasting love; therefore with loving kindness have I drawn thee."

But even this happy note fails to tell the whole story. For the apostle declared: "Whom he did predestinate, them he also called; and whom he called; them he also justified; and whom he justified, them he also glorified."

P stands for the Perseverance of the saints. Some of our Baptist friends refer to this doctrine as the eternal security of the believer. Actually, it should probably be called the *preservation* of the saints. For it teaches that saints on Earth will one day become saints in Heaven. Once a man is saved, he can never be lost. Or as Paul put it: "He which hath begun a good work in you will perform it until the day of Jesus Christ" (Philippians 1: 6).

There may be those times, as we have said, when the staunchest believer is torn by fears and doubts. He may just not "feel saved." But in those darker moments, which we all experience, there comes the sure comfort of Jesus Christ Himself: "My sheep hear my voice, and I know them, and they follow me: And I give unto them eternal life; and they shall never perish, neither shall any man pluck them out of my hand. My Father, which gave them me, is greater than all; and no man is able to pluck them out of my Father's hand. I and my Father are one" (John

10: 27-30).

This does not mean that the elect are better than other men. They are, like the prodigal son, no more than mere beggars for the grace of God. But like the prodigal, though they spend time in the far country, they still remain sons. They "are sanctified by God the Father, and *preserved* in Jesus Christ" (Jude 1).

> Through many dangers, toils and snares,
>   I have already come;
> 'Tis grace hath brought me safe thus far,
> And grace will lead me home.

That is why John Calvin thought of predestination as a "comforting doctrine." Against the fatalism of the world, says Dr. Smith, the sturdy meat-and-potatoes theology of the great Reformer offers an antidote for the deterministic philosophies of the present age.

"It relates (men and history) to the eternities past and to come," he writes. "The obscurest task in life is ennobled by the thought that it is a thread in the warp and woof of that divine purpose at which we are ever weaving in the ceaseless loom of time . . . Every burden, every bereavement, every sorrow, has been foreseen and fore-appointed by a wisdom that cannot err and by a love that cannot change."

> That every cloud, that spreads above
> And veileth love, itself is love.

12

Heirs of the Promises

WEE JOHN DOUGLAS let out a loud bawl as Jack and Arlene Scott approached their pastor standing with a ruling elder beside the baptismal font.

The minister smiled, then raised his voice over another loud wail of a mighty uncomfortable three-month-old and his equally uncomfortable parents.

Both the pastor and the congregation would have been disappointed if little John Douglas hadn't followed the unwritten script.

But a well-aimed bottle of warm milk allowed the minister to get on with the service.

"The mercy of the Lord," the pastor declared, "is from everlasting to everlasting upon them that fear Him, and His righteousness unto children's children;

"To such as keep His covenant, and to those that remember His commandments to do them . . .

"For the promise is unto you, and to your children

and to all that are afar off, even as many as the Lord our God shall call."

How often Grandma and Grandpa Scott had heard those words. They brought back memories of an old stone church outside Glasgow. But now they took on special meaning as John Douglas squirmed uncomfortably in that very unboyish baptismal dress that came lace and all from Scotland.

However, some visitors in the congregation that morning were not as understandably impressed.

There were the Roman Catholic friends of the Scotts who dropped into the service after early mass to witness the baptism of little John Douglas. Apart from some doubt about the validity of the Protestant sacraments, they assumed that baptism conferred divine grace and removed the stain of original sin.

Not a few people, some Presbyterians among them, thought that some kind of magic was involved in the rite, assuring the little fellow a free ticket from Earth to Heaven. Others simply thought that it was the "proper" thing to do—even if the parents only darkened the church door at Christmas and Easter.

It was for these very reasons that a deeply committed Baptist visitor witnessed the proceedings with serious misgivings. He believed that this sacrament (or ordinance, as he called it) was reserved only for young people and adults who had already made a public profession of their faith in Jesus Christ as Savior and Lord.

And, right now, all John Douglas was doing was letting out a loud bellow to give voice to his discomfort.

Why, then, baptize babies?

To answer that question, we first must consider the Presbyterian understanding of the meaning of the sacraments.

"The highest cannot be spoken," said Goethe. "It can only be acted."

145

In the celebration of the Lord's Supper, we therefore re-enact the *drama* of Christ's sacrifice for us at Calvary. Similarly, baptism testifies to the fact that we have become heirs of the promises and children of the covenant which a gracious God established in Christ.

The reformers further understood these sacraments to be *signs,* but, as J. S. Whale points out, "never bare signs or mere illustrations. They are signs whereby the Holy Spirit inwardly affects us," he says. ". . . God Himself sacramentally unites the symbolic action and the grace which it conveys."

Therefore, as most Protestants would agree, the sacraments are a "means of grace"—an outward sign of an inward experience.

However, Presbyterians have always insisted that Word and sacrament go together. "The preaching of the Gospel and the administration of the Gospel sacraments are of Christ's institution," says Dr. Whale. "To exalt one above the other would be to disobey Him whose means of grace they are."

"Prayer is a gift and a sacrifice that we make," says P. T. Forsyth. "Sacrament is a gift and a sacrifice that God makes. In prayer we go to God; in sacrament God comes to us."

The Roman Catholic Church has always insisted that there are seven sacraments—baptism, confirmation, the Lord's Supper, penance, extreme unction, holy orders, and matrimony. A popular manual of Catholic teaching comments:

Baptism was instituted to impart grace the first time; penance to restore it, if lost by sin; and the other five sacraments to intensify the life of sanctifying grace already possessed.

Since baptism and penance give supernatural life to persons "dead" in sin, they are called sacraments of the dead. The other sacraments strengthen the supernatural life of persons already living in the state of grace, so they are called sacraments of the living. Anyone who knowingly receives a sacrament of the living while guilty of mortal sin commits a mortal sin of sacrilege because he treats a sacred thing with grave irreverence.

In reply, Protestants would first insist that all sin is mortal. They make no distinction between "little" (or venial) sins and "big" (mortal) ones. For the Bible simply declares: "The soul that sinneth, it shall die" (Ezekiel 18: 4, 20).

At the same time, the Protestant rejoices in the knowledge that, while "the wages of sin is death," the "gift of God is eternal life through Jesus Christ our Lord" (Romans 6: 23). "For there is one God, and one mediator between God and men," says Paul, "the man Christ Jesus" (I Timothy 2: 5).

But this firm declaration concerning the relationship between Christ and the Christian inevitably brings up the question of how the grace of Christ is mediated and applied. Surprisingly, Calvin took a pronounced "catholic" view of this matter.

"Our first entrance . . . into the Church and Kingdom of God," says Calvin, "is the remission of sins, without which we have no covenant or union with God . . .

"Nor does God only once receive and adopt us into His Church by the remission of sins," he says. "He likewise preserves and keeps us in it by the same mercy.

"Wherefore it ought to be held as a *certain* conclusion," he writes, "that from the Divine liberality, by the intervention of the *merit* of Christ, through the *sanctification* of the Spirit, pardon of sins has been, and is daily, bestowed upon us, who have been admitted and ingrafted into the *body* of the Church."

While the preaching of the Word and the administration of the sacraments has been entrusted to pastors and ministers, says Calvin, the "power of the keys" has been "conferred on the society of believers." "Let every one of us, therefore, consider it as his duty," he concludes, "not to seek remission of sins anywhere but where the Lord has placed it."

At the same time, the reformers denied the notion that there were seven sacraments. The *Scots Confession,* for example, spoke for all Protestants when it affirmed that only two sacraments "alone were instituted *by the Lord Jesus* and commanded to be used by all who will be counted members of His Body, that is, Baptism and the Supper or Table of the Lord Jesus, also called the Communion of His Body and Blood."

These two sacraments instituted by Christ, like the Old Testament rites of circumcision and the Passover, says the *Scots Confession,* were intended "by God not only to make a visible distinction between His people and those who were without the Covenant, but also to exercise the faith of His children and, by participation of these sacraments, to seal in their hearts the assurance of His promise, and of that most blessed . . . union . . . which the chosen have with their Head, Christ Jesus."

It is not surprising, therefore, that this confession "utterly condemn(ed)" the Anabaptist "vanity" that the sacraments were no more than "naked and bare signs."

But the *Scots Confession,* like other Reformed creeds, departed from the Roman Catholic notion that there was some sort of intrinsic merit or grace in the sacramental elements themselves.

"We readily admit that we make a distinction between Christ Jesus in His eternal substance and the elements of the sacramental signs," it declared. "So we neither worship the elements, in place of that which they signify, nor yet do we despise them or undervalue them."

The *Scots Confession* rather recognized that the sacraments were to be observed with reverence and that those who receive the Lord's Supper must first examine themselves "diligently." For the apostle declared:

> Wherefore whosoever shall eat this bread, and drink this cup of the Lord, unworthily, shall be guilty of the body and blood of the Lord. But let a man examine himself, and so let him eat of that bread, and drink of that cup. For he that eateth and drinketh unworthily, eateth and drinketh damnation to himself, not discerning the Lord's body (I Corinthians 11: 27-29).

"We hold that baptism applies as much to the *children of the faithful* as to those who are of age and discretion," declares the *Scots Confession,* "and so we condemn the error of the Anabaptists, who deny that children should be baptized before they have faith and understanding.

"But we hold that the Supper of the Lord is only for those who are of the household of faith and can try and examine themselves both in their faith and their duty to their neighbors," it further affirms.

"Those who eat and drink at that holy table without faith, or without peace and goodwill to their brethren, eat unworthily," it says. "This is the reason why ministers in our Kirk make public and individual examination of those who are to be admitted to the table of the Lord Jesus."

But this does not mean that other Christians are excluded from receiving this sacrament in Presbyterian churches. For they recognize that this is not the Presbyterian table but rather the Lord's Table. And so they practice *open communion,* inviting all who sincerely put their faith and confidence in Jesus Christ to join in the sacred meal.

"The Table of Christ is a family table," says McCheyne, "spread in this wilderness, and none of the *true children* should be absent from it, or be separated while sitting at it."

"The main thing is not the sacramental action in its

manward aspect, but in its Godward aspect," says Dr. Whale. "In the sacraments we have effectual signs of God acting."

This means that the administration of the sacraments does not depend upon the character of the minister himself. "Neither does the efficacy of a sacrament depend upon the piety or intention of him that doth administer it," says the *Westminster Confession,* "but upon the work of the Spirit and the Word of institution."

With that in mind, let's turn to a closer look at baptism and the Lord's Supper.

The Baptists insist—and with no little persuasion—that to be a Christian a man or woman must believe in the deity of Jesus Christ, as well as in His sacrificial death and glorious resurrection. Therefore, they see baptism as that ordinance in which the believer is "buried with him in baptism . . . [and] risen with him through the faith of the operation of God, who hath raised him from the dead" (Colossians 2: 12).

It is impossible for a baby to demonstrate responsive faith, they say. Therefore, infant baptism is meaningless and worse.

But almost all other Christian communions share the conviction that here the Baptists miss the crucial point. What is important in baptism is not only our faith but God's gracious and saving action on our behalf long before we even knew of our lost and needy condition.

Infant baptism testifies to the *objective fact* of our redemption, says Dr. Whale, "at that point in human life where no *subjective response* to it is possible on the part of the baptized individual."

To paraphrase President Kennedy, it's not so much a matter of our faith in God as it is a demonstration of God's redemptive love for His own elect.

"Baptism is neither an act of dedication in which the main thing is what the celebrants do," says Dr. Whale, "nor is it a magic rite effecting regeneration.

"The child is baptized by Christ," he says, "into His Church, the household of faith."

This means that the faith demonstrated in infant baptism is not that of the child but that of the church. It is for this reason that the minister delivers this charge to the entire congregation, rather than to so-called "Godparents":

This child is now received into Christ's Church: And you *the people of this congregation* in receiving this child promise with God's help to be *his* (her) *sponsor* to the end that he (she) may confess Christ as his (her) Lord and Saviour and come at last to His eternal Kingdom. Jesus said, Whoso shall receive one such little child in My Name receiveth Me.

But this certainly does not mean that this is the end of the matter. The congregation is then entrusted with the awesome responsibility of providing an atmosphere of tender loving care and adequate Christian education as befits an heir of the promises and a child of the covenant.

Moreover, the time comes in the life of the child himself when he is called upon to *publicly confirm* the vows taken for him in infancy. After a prolonged period of study with the pastor, he stands before the entire congregation and is expected to answer the following questions affirmatively before becoming a communicant member of the church:

Do you *confirm* the vows taken for you in baptism and with a humble and contrite heart put your whole trust in the mercy of God, which is in Christ Jesus our Lord?

Do you promise to make diligent use of the means of grace, to share faithfully in the worship and service of the Church, to give of your substance as the Lord may prosper you, and to give your whole heart to the service of Christ and His Kingdom throughout the world?

151

The United Presbyterian *Book of Order* admonishes pastors to meet with the parents before the baptism of their child "to acquaint them with the significance of what God is doing in this act and with the responsibilities which it lays upon them.

"At least one parent, or one rightly exercising parental authority," says *The Book of Order,* "shall be asked to make affirmation of faith in Jesus Christ as Lord and Savior. He shall also promise publicly, in dependence on the grace of God, to raise the child to love God and serve Him, to the end that the child may come to confess Jesus Christ as Lord and Savior."

For Presbyterians recognize and teach that no one *inherits* the new life in Christ on the basis of his parents' faith. Or, as Catherine Marshall so aptly put it, God has no grandchildren. Rather each individual is born into the Kingdom of God by an act of personal faith and commitment to Jesus Christ. "Ye must be born again!"

Meanwhile, Presbyterians have traditionally baptized their young by sprinkling. But they accept into communicant membership any Christian who has been baptized in the saving Name of the Father, the Son, and the Holy Spirit, no matter what the mode of baptism itself. (The author's sons, Paul and Timothy, have had the good fortune of having a father who was wise and fortunate enough to marry a good Baptist girl. While Paul was baptized in the traditional Presbyterian manner, Timmy was immersed by his own dad in the River Jordan at the point where the river meets the Sea of Galilee. Two Glen Morris ruling elders were present along with a onetime Baptist mom. And the baptismal certificate was graciously provided by the Anglican Diocese of Jerusalem!)

What is important, says *The Book of Order,* is that the whole worshiping community recognize that they themselves are "likewise . . . helpless children, whom God in His mercy has called to eternal life in the Spirit."

While baptism has sometimes been called the "sacrament of unity," the Lord's Supper has sadly testified to our division. In fact, some of the most heated theological battles have been fought at the Table of our one Lord and Savior.

At the time of the Reformation, there was universal Protestant reaction against the Roman dogma of *transubstantiation,* which holds that the bread and wine are transformed into the very body and very blood of Christ. The Roman Catholic Church took this position on dubious Scriptural grounds and then attempted to explain the dogma on the basis of equally dubious philosophical speculation.

In the Protestant camp, Luther advanced the notion of *consubstantiation* as his answer to the Roman doctrine of the *eternal sacrifice* of the mass. While this view is now rejected by many Lutheran theologians, it is enough to say that Luther sought to protect the integrity of the "real presence" of Christ at His own Table.

Meanwhile, Zwingli and the Anabaptists broke completely with any notion of the "real presence" and insisted that the Lord's Supper represented the *faithful remembrance* of that sacrifice which Christ made once for all. Baptists still emphasize this *memorial* aspect of the communion meal, which for them is, like baptism, an ordinance and not a sacrament.

Against these competing claims the Presbyterians sought to incorporate into their understanding of Holy Communion the various teachings of Scripture on this most sacred matter. So it was that the *Scots Confession* declared:

> . . . In the Supper rightly used, Christ Jesus is so joined with us that He becomes the *very nourishment* and food of our souls. Not that we imagine any transubstantiation of bread into Christ's body, and of wine into His natural blood, as the Romanists

have perniciously taught and wrongly believed; but this union . . . which we have with the body and blood of Christ Jesus in the right use of the sacraments is wrought by means of the Holy Ghost who by true faith carries us above all things that are visible, carnal, and earthly, and makes us feed upon the body and blood of Christ Jesus, *once broken and shed* for us but now in heaven, and appearing for us in the presence of His Father . . . Therefore, if anyone slanders us by saying that we affirm or believe the sacraments to be symbols and nothing more, they are libelous and speak against the plain facts . . .

So it is that when Presbyterians gather around the Table of their Lord they believe they are participating in the drama of Christ's sacrificial and atoning death on Calvary's Cross. As McCheyne suggested:

1. We remember the time when it was instituted—the very night in which He was betrayed. "It was the darkest night that ever was in this world, and yet the brightest—the night when His love to sinners was put to the severest test. How amazing that He should remember our comfort at such a time."

2. We believe that it is the sacrament for Christians only. "The Lord's Supper is the children's bread; it is intended only for those who know and love the Lord Jesus."

3. We rejoice that Christ is the beginning, middle and end of it. "This do in remembrance of Me." "Ye do show the Lord's death till He come." "Christ is the Alpha and Omega of the Lord's Supper; it is Christ and Him crucified. These give a sweetness to the bread and wine."

But we also believe with John Calvin that "our souls are fed by the flesh and blood of Christ in the same way that bread and wine keep and sustain physical life." For our blessed Savior Himself declared: "I am the bread of life: he that cometh to me shall never hunger; and he that believeth on me shall never thirst. . . . him that cometh to me I will in no wise cast out" (John 6: 35, 37).

That is the Divine invitation. He awaits your personal response.

> There for me the Savior stands,
>> Holding forth His wounded hands;
> God is Love! I know, I feel,
>> Jesus weeps and loves me still.

Questions for Discussion

1. RAPPING WITH REBELS

1. Was John Witherspoon wrong to mix religion and politics?
2. Was there a Biblical basis for separation of church and state?
3. Are Christians permitted to fight in a just war? What illustrations can you find in the Old and New Testaments to support your position?
4. What has happened in history whenever one church has become the established church of the state?
5. On what spiritual foundations did the early Republic rest?
6. Is America today living up to its spiritual heritage? If not, why not? And what can be done about it?

2. THE VOICE OF THE PEOPLE

1. Does faith mean the death of reason? Can a Christian accept truth from whatever source it might come? Why?
2. Do Calvin's troubles with the people in Geneva tell us anything about troubles in the churches today?
3. Would you have liked to live in Calvin's Geneva?
4. What "authority," if any, must a minister possess if he is to carry on his ministry effectively? From where does this authority come?
5. Do you think discipline—even excommunication—is necessary in Protestant churches today?
6. Was Calvin right to demand separation of church and state?

3. KNOCKING WITH KNOX

1. Does that crash course in French that Knox took aboard that galley ship have anything to tell us about God's providence? Check Romans 8.
2. Is it true, as many people claim, that religion is divisive and has caused more wars than any other single historical factor? If this is so, why?
3. Should the state oversee the affairs of the church?
4. Can faith be separated from works? Check Ephesians and James.
5. What is the true basis for "law and order"?
6. Should the Christian oppose duly constituted civil authority? If so, under what conditions?

4. DEBATING WITH THE DARING

1. To whom did Caracciolo owe his primary loyalty? To Christ or his family? Check the Gospels.
2. They say, "Rome never changes." Do you think this is true since Vatican II?
3. Have Protestants always been right?
4. Do you see any connection between a nation which rejects the Gospel and that nation facing bloodshed as in the case of the French Revolution? Can you think of some Old Testament illustrations? What lessons are there for us today?
5. Does the Bible and church history have anything to say about "bleacher believers" and "sideline Christianity"?
6. They say Northern Ireland is a country with "a lot of religion and no Christianity." If this is true, where did the problem arise and what may be the answer to the so-called "Irish Question"?

5. WANDERING IN THE WILDERNESS

1. Is popularity always to be regarded as a Christian virtue?
2. How would you reconcile the differences of opinion between those who championed an educated ministry over against those who argued for evangelism at any cost? Is Christ always honored by zeal above knowledge?

3. Was the union of the Congregationalists and the Presbyterians a good thing? Or did the later division cause more harm than good in the long run? What is the basis for Christian unity? And what generally happens when churches become divided? Can you cite any Scriptural references?
4. Were the Northern Presbyterians wrong to introduce the Gardener Spring resolutions? Should the church dabble in politics? What about Calvin and Knox?
5. How would you, Yankee or Rebel, assess the Christian convictions of Abraham Lincoln? What was less Christian—slavery or war?
6. Can a man still be a Christian in a scientific age?

6. Sign in, Please

1. Can you find the names of the following churches in the New Testament—Methodist, Baptist, Lutheran, Episcopal or Catholic? Search the Scriptures!
2. On what various bases did Protestant bodies get their names?
3. What strengths and/or weaknesses do you see in a congregational form of church government?
4. Ditto on the episcopal type?
5. Where could the pastor, ruling elders and deacons in your church improve their style of ministry?
6. Should the presbytery, synod and general assembly speak to or for all Presbyterians?

7. Thinking God's Thoughts After Him

1. Is Christian faith only for old people, something you put off until you "stand upon the brink of eternity"?
2. What about the comment, "A God who could be proved would be no God at all"?
3. Do you see any personal value in the so-called classical arguments for the existence of God? How, if ever, might they be put to good use?
4. Do you think you could retain your faith after seeing the bloodshed of war? Spending long years in a POW camp? Losing a baby? Or your home? Or your job?
5. What was Calvin trying to get at, after all?
6. Is your God too small?

8. BACK TO THE BIBLE

1. Does the Bible speak God's Word to you? How does it become a living Book?
2. How would you react to the charge that the Bible is unscientific and filled with the myths and legends of an ancient people?
3. Can you depend upon Scripture to be scientifically and/or historically accurate?
4. Can you criticize the Bible as you would a book by Shakespeare or Browning?
5. Is the Bible the Word of God or does it merely contain the Word of God?
6. Do you consider the Bible to still be "the only infallible rule for faith and practice"?

9. CHRISTIANS ANONYMOUS?

1. Is the church a hospital for sinners or a museum for saints?
2. A medieval proverb says: "The church is something like Noah's Ark. If it wasn't for the storm without, you couldn't stand the smell within." What's your comment?
3. Are doctrinal differences silly? Or are there valid reasons for them?
4. Are different denominations an asset or liability for the cause of Christ?
5. What is the primary basis for unity among Christians?
6. Is the Presbyterian Church the "true" church? Is it Catholic or Reformed? Or both?

10. DO YOU ACCEPT THE OFFER?

1. Someone has said that history is His Story. In what sense is this true?
2. Does our belief in the Trinity mean that we worship "Three Gods"? Is Jesus a lesser God than the Father? Is the Holy Spirit merely an influence or power? Search the Scriptures.
3. Can a man be "saved" by the example of Jesus Christ?
4. Does God wait until we are "good enough" to offer us His salvation in Christ?
5. Are there times when you "don't feel saved"? What's

God's answer to this common complaint?

6. Do you know Jesus Christ as your personal Lord and Savior?

11. HAVE YOU BEEN ELECTED?

1. Do you think Calvin did teach that "whatever will be, will be"?

2. Would you make a better Arminian than a Calvinist? Do you believe, for example, in "total depravity" and that man cannot resist the grace of God? Or that "once saved, always saved"?

3. Does Calvinism promote despair or realistic optimism? Are we optimistic about man climbing ever upward and onward?

4. What would you say to the person who says he is out for his "kicks"?

5. Do you think church members are better than other people? Who is really righteous?

6. Have you ever felt that God has let you down? Or has He shown that He really cares for you?

12. PROMISES, PROMISES

1. Is there some kind of magic in baptism and the Lord's Supper?

2. Are the sacraments merely interesting traditions of the church?

3. Does baptism wash away the stain of original sin?

4. Or are the Baptists right to insist in "believers' baptism" by total immersion? What mode of baptism do you favor? Why?

5. Have you ever felt the spiritual presence of Christ in you when you received the Lord's Supper?

6. Do you believe you are one of the "elect" and an heir of the promises?

REACH OUT
with additional copies of this book...

Simply ask for them at your local bookstore—or order from the David C. Cook Publishing Co., Elgin, IL 60120 (in Canada: Weston, Ont. M9L 1T4).